Superfood or Superthreat

Titles in the Issues in Focus Today *series:*

Addictions and Risky Behaviors
Cutting, Bingeing, Snorting, and Other Dangers
ISBN-13: 978-0-7660-2165-5
ISBN-10:   0-7660-2165-3

Am I Fat?
The Obesity Issue for Teens
ISBN-13: 978-0-7660-2527-1
ISBN-10:   0-7660-2527-6

Attack of the Superbugs
The Crisis of Drug-Resistant Diseases
ISBN-13: 978-0-7660-2400-7
ISBN-10:   0-7660-2400-8

Bioethics
Who Lives, Who Dies, and Who Decides?
ISBN-13: 978-0-7660-2546-2
ISBN-10:   0-7660-2546-2

Bullying
How to Deal With Taunting, Teasing, and Tormenting
ISBN-13: 978-0-7660-2355-0
ISBN-10:   0-7660-2355-9

Dating, Relationships, and Sexuality
What Teens Should Know
ISBN-13: 978-0-7660-1948-5
ISBN-10:   0-7660-1948-9

Downloading Copyrighted Stuff From the Internet
Stealing or Fair Use?
ISBN-13: 978-0-7660-2164-8
ISBN-10:   0-7660-2164-5

High-Tech Babies
The Debate Over Assisted Reproductive Technology
ISBN-13: 978-0-7660-2528-8
ISBN-10:   0-7660-2528-4

Other People's Words
What Plagiarism Is and How to Avoid It
ISBN-13: 978-0-7660-2525-7
ISBN-10:   0-7660-2525-X

Peanut Butter, Milk, and Other Deadly Threats
What You Should Know About Food Allergies
ISBN-13: 978-0-7660-2529-5
ISBN-10:   0-7660-2529-2

Resolving Conflicts
How to Get Along When You Don't Get Along
ISBN-13: 978-0-7660-2359-8
ISBN-10:   0-7660-2359-1

The Stem Cell Debate
The Ethics and Science Behind the Research
ISBN-13: 978-0-7660-2545-5
ISBN-10:   0-7660-2545-4

Superfood or Superthreat
The Issue of Genetically Engineered Food
ISBN-13: 978-0-7660-2681-0
ISBN-10:   0-7660-2681-7

You Have the Right to Know Your Rights
What Teens Should Know
ISBN-13: 978-0-7660-2358-1
ISBN-10:   0-7660-2358-3

Superfood or Superthreat
The Issue of Genetically Engineered Food

ISSUES IN FOCUS TODAY

Kathlyn Gay

Enslow Publishers, Inc.
40 Industrial Road
Box 398
Berkeley Heights, NJ 07922
USA

http://www.enslow.com

Library of Congress Cataloging-in-Publication Data

Gay, Kathlyn.
    Superfood or superthreat : the issue of genetically engineered food / Kathlyn Gay.
      p. cm. — (Issues in focus today)
    Includes bibliographical references and index.
    ISBN-13: 978-0-7660-2681-0
    ISBN-10: 0-7660-2681-7
    1. Genetically modified foods. 2. Food—Biotechnology. I. Title.
    TP248.65.F66G39 2006
    363.19'2—dc22

                                2006021070

Printed in the United States of America

10 9 8 7 6 5 4 3 2 1

To Our Readers: We have done our best to make sure that all Internet Addresses in this book
were active and appropriate when we went to press. However, the author and publisher have
no control over and assume no liability for the material available on those Internet sites or on
other Web sites they may link to. Any comments or suggestions can be sent by e-mail to
comments@enslow.com or to the address on the back cover.

Illustration Credits: AP/Wide World, p. 5, 36, 38, 47, 51, 61, 64, 74, 76, 81, 99, 103;
Stephen Ausmus, Agricultural Research Service/U.S. Department of Agriculture (ARS/
USDA), pp. 5, 24, 53, 101; Scott Bauer, ARS/USDA, pp. 10, 15, 84, 95, 97; Jack Dykinga,
ARS/USDA, pp. 3, 5, 27, 57; Peggy Greb, ARS/USDA, pp. 5, 70; Photos.com, pp. 5, 17, 20,
31, 86, 89, 92; Shutterstock, pp. 5, 7, 66, 105; Keith Weller, ARS/USDA, p. 43.

Cover Illustration: Stephen Ausmus, ARS/USDA (large photo); BananaStock (small photo)

Contents

Chapter 1 What's in a Name?   7

Chapter 2 The First Modified Foods   17

Chapter 3 Production of GE Food   27

Chapter 4 Opposing and Protesting GE Products   38

Chapter 5 Reaping the Benefits of GMOs   53

Chapter 6 Regulating GE Crops   66

Chapter 7 The Politics of GMOs   76

Chapter 8 Consumer Views and Choices   86

Chapter Notes   95

Glossary   106

For More Information   108

Further Reading and
Internet Addresses   109

Index   110

What's in a Name?

If it waddles like a pig, eats like a pig, and smells like a pig, it's a pig, right? Well, yes, except that there is a special breed of pig that looks like the ordinary farmyard variety but was modified by scientists in a Canadian laboratory. That was in the late 1990s, and ever since then, researchers have been testing this line of new pigs, a breed known by the trademarked name "Enviropig." The name stems from the fact that the animal's waste is "environmentally friendly."

Does that mean that pig poop no longer stinks? No. It still has a strong odor just like the ordinary variety of pig manure. And the odor of that ordinary variety can be overpowering if you live in a rural area near an industrial hog farm that raises thousands of pigs. In the Midwest and Southeast hog-producing states, as well as in rural Canada, it is not unusual for neighbors of hog producers to complain that some days they cannot go outdoors because the smell of the manure buildup is so bad. It can make a person nauseated.

However, there is another problem with manure from industrial hog farms. It is stored in large open-air lagoons, and then sprayed as fertilizer on nearby fields. In a state like North Carolina that has 10 million hogs, the animals excrete "twice as much feces and urine as the populations of the cities of Los Angeles, New York and Chicago combined," according to a report on public broadcasting's *Online NewsHour.*[1] Ordinary pig manure as fertilizer has a high concentration of phosphorous that can leach into groundwater or run off the land into streams, rivers, and lakes. Phosphorous is an essential nutrient for plant growth, but excess phosphorous causes widespread growth of algae and plants in waterways, taking up the oxygen that fish and other aquatic life need for survival.

The Enviropig, by contrast, excretes waste that is lower in phosphorous than that of a conventional pig or hog (the two words are synonymous in the United States). With development of the Enviropig, researchers hope that large-scale hog producers in North America as well as elsewhere will be able to raise this new breed without endangering water resources. However, in some regions the total amount of phosphorus pollution may determine how many hogs are raised, thus switching to Enviropigs could allow hog farms to raise even more pigs, creating other types of pollutants. Also, there is no certainty that consumers will accept and eat "enviro pork."

The uncertainty stems in part from a debate that has been going on in many countries since the 1990s. Scientists, environmentalists, farmers, livestock producers, and the general public argue over the benefits and the risks of genetically engineered (GE) food. Other commonly used terms are biotech food, genetically modified organisms (GMOs), and genetically modified (GM) food.

What Is GE Food?

If you are not familiar with GE food or products, you are not alone. Most Americans know little about GE food, according to surveys conducted by the Rutgers University Food Policy Institute (FPI) in 2002, 2003, and 2004. The American public also admits not knowing what types of GE products are available. In addition, the FPI survey of about twelve hundred people disclosed that respondents were not familiar with the technology and issues involved in creating GE food. Some were concerned, though, about the safety of such products, and large numbers wanted GE foods labeled as such.[2]

Whether from animal or plant sources, scientists create GE food through biotechnology techniques (hence the term biotech foods). If you were to search for "biotech food" on the Internet, you would come up with twice as many hits as you would with the term "GE food." However, the term "biotech" "is almost too broad to be useful," the Union of Concerned Scientists explains. Biotechnology "applies to all practical uses of living organisms—anything from microorganisms used in the fermentation of beer to the most sophisticated application of gene therapy."[3]

Transferring Genes

For GE food, scientists transfer genes from one organism to another, creating an organism that is genetically different from a preexisting plant or animal. The process may be called genetic modification, transgenic technology, or recombinant DNA (rDNA). For the most part, this book will use the terms GE foods or GMOs.

Creating GMOs became possible when scientists in the 1970s successfully transferred deoxyribonucleic acid (DNA)

Large-scale hog production is hard on water quality. The Enviropig was developed to address this problem.

from one life form to another. The molecule DNA is part of the chromosome structure of cells. It is like a communication system that holds all the coded instructions required to make an organism. The DNA molecule is composed of sugar, phosphate, and four nitrogen bases, adenine (A), thymine (T), guanine (G), and cystosine (C). Together, the sugar, phosphate, and bases make up a nucleotide. The four bases are always paired in the same way: A with T and G with C. Sugar and phosphate connect the pairs, linked together in long chains twisted in a double helix—something like a corkscrew ladder. A group of base pairs on a strand of DNA makes up a gene. The instructions contained in genes are codes for making proteins, the building blocks that determine, in conjunction with the environment, the characteristics of all living things. To transfer traits from one organism to another, scientists remove desired genes from a plant or animal cell and insert them into the genetic material of another plant or animal.

> **For GE food, scientists transfer genes from one organism to another, creating an organism that is genetically different from a preexisting plant or animal.**

Methods of Gene Transfer in Plants

When transferring genes in plants, scientists essentially add a new protein to an organism. Some proteins are enzymes— natural substances—that act as catalysts, or agents, to make a reaction occur. Other proteins help build cells and tissues. Scientists use biotechnology tools to insert a gene into a plant to give it a specific new characteristic. "Once in the plant, the new gene does what all genes do: It directs the production of a specific protein that makes the plant uniquely different," the U.S. Food and Drug Administration explained. "This technology provides much more control over, and precision to, what characteristic breeders give to a new plant."[4]

In a common gene transfer procedure, one enzyme works like chemical scissors to snip away a specific piece of DNA, and then another enzyme acts like glue and pastes the piece into the DNA of another organism such as a virus or small piece of genetic material (called plasmid) in bacterium. Bacteria and viruses serve as carriers—they transfer the DNA to the recipient or host.

For example, some bacteria naturally produce a toxin that is lethal to plant insects, and the gene for that toxin can be removed and placed into the genetic material of another organism. FPI at Rutgers University explains it this way:

> Scientists isolate the desired gene in the DNA of one organism, extract it, then insert it into the DNA of another organism's seed. When the seed grows and its cells divide, each cell contains the new gene. Hence, whatever trait that gene expressed in the original organism is now a part of the new organism. . . . The new organism is genetically distinct and different from its original predecessor.[5]

Another method of transfer is called microinjection, in which technicians use a small needle to inject genetic material into a recipient cell. A projectile technique called bioballistics might also be used. Laboratory experts coat tiny slivers of metal (such as gold) with genetic material and then use a device informally known as a "gene gun" to shoot the new genes into the nucleus of a cell.

How the Enviropig Got Here

Developing a GE animal like the Enviropig is not quite the same as genetically engineering a plant. In 1999, scientists at the University of Guelph in Ontario, Canada, transferred genes from a mouse into a common intestinal bacterium, *Escherichia coli (E. coli)*, and inserted this newly formed gene (called a transgene) into more than four thousand embryos (fertilized eggs) of Yorkshire pigs. The gene took hold in only one percent

Early Gene Transfer

One early result of gene transfer is an artificial hormone called recombinant bovine somatotropin, or rbST, approved by the FDA in 1993 after extensive testing by medical and scientific organizations. Bovine somatotropin (bST) or bovine growth hormone (BGH), as it is also called, is a hormone produced naturally in the pituitary glands of cows and other animals. It is essential for normal growth, development, and health maintenance. Dairy farmers use the genetically modified hormone rbST, injecting it into cows so that the animals will produce more milk than they would normally without the artificial hormone. The hormone does not modify the DNA of cows. But animal welfare and environmental groups strongly oppose the practice, arguing that it interferes with the cow's natural physiology and endangers the animal's health. On the other hand, such authorities as the American Medical Association and the National Institutes of Health say that the cows and their milk as well as meat from the animals treated with the artificial hormone are as safe as those from untreated cows.

of the embryos, which researchers then transplanted into sows (female pigs) that gave birth to the new breed.

The new pigs, with the aid of the transgene, were able to produce an enzyme called *phytase* in their salivary glands, which allows them to digest phytate. Phytate is a form of phosphorous that occurs naturally in plants like corn, barley, wheat, and soybean meal used for animal feed, but it is an indigestible form of phosphate. Ordinary pigs excrete it in waste, so they are fed expensive supplements that enable them to maintain the best possible growth and development for market. Because the Enviropigs digest the phosphorous in their feed more efficiently than ordinary pigs, they not only can benefit the environment but can also reduce costs for producers who no longer would have to add supplements to their pigs' diets.[6]

By early 2005, Guelph scientists presented data about the phosphorous-absorbing pigs to Canadian and U.S. regulatory agencies that determine the safety of foods. But to date, neither country has a process for approving or monitoring the new breed of pigs. Thus, it is not known when or if the new pig will go to market.

Actually, no GE food animals have been approved for sale in the United States, although a small number of other farm and laboratory animals have been modified. GE salmon, for example, have been engineered to grow at least twice as fast as those in the wild, presenting the possibility of getting the fish to market in a much shorter time period.

GE Crops

Without a doubt, the major GE foods come from plants. The first genetically modified plants were developed to produce insecticides that do not harm people but kill insects that destroy crops. These GE plants were field-tested in 1985 in the United States. By 1995, the U.S. Environmental Protection Agency (EPA) had approved commercial planting of GE plants known as Bt crops. Bt stands for *Bacillus thuringiensis*, a toxin that kills pests like the corn borer, a caterpillar that damages more than one billion dollars' worth of crops each year.[7]

Bt is found naturally in the soil. Since World War II, it has been used in the United States to produce alternatives to chemical pesticides. Bt pesticides are target specific; that is, they are designed for particular insect pests, such as moths, caterpillars, and beetles. Pests ingest the toxin, which creates holes in the digestive tract and allows bacteria to enter the body. Within hours, insects stop feeding on treated plants; they die in about two days.

During the 1980s, Bt use increased because insects became resistant to synthetic insecticides. Governments and private manufacturers began to research plants that could be engineered to produce their own Bt. By 1995, Bt corn became the first plant with the built-in toxin to be registered with the EPA.

These berries are not genetically engineered, but they have been selectively bred by scientists to survive in different conditions so they can be grown more widely.

Bt crops—corn, cotton, and potatoes—have been engineered to produce their own toxin, which kills the pests that destroy the crops. Other GE plants are designed to resist herbicides, or weed killers. When herbicides are sprayed on fields, the GE crop plants that have built-in protection or tolerance (often called HT crops) are not destroyed along with the weeds.

Some GE crops are designed to improve their flavor. An example is the Flavr Savr tomato, marketed in the mid-1990s.

It was modified to stay on the vine to ripen, allowing it to develop more flavor than ordinary tomatoes, which are picked green and often ripened with ethylene gas. The GE tomato was also engineered to reduce spoilage after harvesting. But the tomatoes damaged easily while being transported, and the developer, Calgene, withdrew the product from the market in 1997. Nevertheless, Calgene and several other companies are developing new varieties of GE tomatoes, hoping to bring them to market in the near future.

Some GE plants have been enhanced with vitamins and minerals, while others have been developed to grow in poor soil conditions. Still others are specifically engineered to produce pharmaceuticals—drugs to treat diseases—which could be helpful in countries where preventive medications are not readily available.

Today, the main genetically modified organisms produced and marketed in the United States are crop plants such as corn, soybeans, cotton, and rapeseed (from which canola oil is derived). In Canada, where most of the canola used in the United States is actually produced, 60 percent of the rapeseed crop is genetically modified, while in the United States more than 80 percent of soybean crops and 40 percent of corn are GE varieties.[8]

GE corn, canola, cottonseed oil, and soy are the most common GE ingredients used in processed foods—manufactured foods such as frozen dinners, cereals, snacks, cooking oils, margarine, flour, products with corn syrup, and many more. In the United States, most processed foods—from 60 to 80 percent—have a genetically engineered ingredient.[9] Long before GE food products made it to supermarket shelves, however, discoveries by plant and animal breeders of the past laid the foundation for biotechnological developments. Ancient people and more recent ancestors paved the way for today's DNA manipulation that changes the nature of many organisms.

The First Modified Foods

Thousands of years before scientists began to transfer genes from one species to another, ancient people were applying biotechnology techniques—if you consider biotechnology in the very broad sense of manipulating organisms for a human purpose. Early people hunted and gathered most of their food but they knew that some natural processes were at work to modify what they ate and drank.

No one knows exactly when fermentation was discovered, but as long as seven thousand years ago, the Sumerians of Mesopotamia were knowledgeable about the fermentation process that produced beer and wine. During fermentation living microorganisms (one-celled organisms) such as bacteria, yeasts, and molds (fungus growths) act on various food ingredients, changing the original product. About 4000 B.C., the Chinese discovered a range of fermentation processes, such as the use of lactic acid bacteria to make yogurt. They also created vinegar and wine, and used molds to produce cheese.

As ancient people in different parts of the world began to make a transition from hunting and gathering food, they started to domesticate, or tame, wild animals and plant crops in a systematic way. Early people, for example, tamed wolves (the ancestors of dogs), goats, sheep, and horses. They bred animals to serve their needs, such as the ox to pull a plow, and the mule, which is the offspring of a male donkey and a female horse, to serve as a pack animal.

In addition, they domesticated plants such as corn, wheat, rice, and some fruits and vegetables. Such food crops originated with wild plants. Consider maize, or corn. Corn, as we know it today, would not have been possible without the indigenous people (American Indians) who cultivated it at least seven thousand years ago in Central America. Researchers were not certain about maize's ancestry, though they had long theorized that it originated from a wild grass called teosinte. Then in 2004, Mary Eubanks, a plant geneticist at Duke University, demonstrated that maize was produced from an accidental cross between teosinte and another wild grass called gamagrass.[1]

A wide range of plants originated from such accidental crosses. In this process, pollen is transferred from one plant to another, often by the wind or insects, fertilizing it, and producing a variation of the plant. Early people were able to improve these plants by selecting the best seeds or vegetative parts, planting them during the next growing season, and caring for them until the harvest. In other words, they practiced agriculture, or farming.

Early Agriculture

It is commonly believed that agriculture began about ten thousand years ago, a concept that is still presented in some academic settings and encyclopedic entries. However, Professor Gordon Hillman of University College London and an archaeological team found that cultivation of cereal crops such as wheat and rye actually began around thirteen thousand years ago. Hillman and his colleagues base their theory on nearly three decades of studying remains of a settlement unearthed in the Euphrates region of Syria. There they found evidence of an extended drought that forced people who relied on wild grasses and seeds for food to cultivate the seeds in order to survive. Hillman says that people took the wild cereal seeds to areas where there was soil moisture to help the plants grow. The cultivated seeds that the team found have proven to be the oldest yet discovered.

Farmers continued to domesticate and selectively breed or modify plants and animals over thousands of years. For example, more than five thousand years ago, the Incas of Peru observed that certain types of potatoes grew better at higher altitudes—14,000 feet rather than at 10,000 feet. So the Peruvians planted potatoes at the elevations where they would grow the best.

Selective breeding and modification of plants and animals certainly took place in North America for many centuries before European explorers came to the continent. In fact, European colonists learned from American Indians how to plant and harvest corn, beans, squash, and other New World crops. Colonial farming—like all farming—depended on human labor and animal power, and that did not change much until the late 1900s, when new technologies and mechanization—motorized farm machinery as opposed to horse- or ox-drawn plows, wagons, and other equipment—eased much of the backbreaking toil of farming and increased efficiency.

People have been plowing with oxen since ancient times. Selective breeding was part of the process of domesticating both plants and animals.

The work of botanists and plant breeders also played a major role in changing and improving agricultural practices. One of those plant breeders was Gregor Mendel, an Austrian monk in Central Europe who taught high school mathematics.

In a Monastery Garden

Gregor Mendel loved nature and began studying and experimenting with plants in attempts to learn how basic characteristics were passed across generations of the same species. His most famous work was conducted in a monastery garden, where from 1856 to 1863, he studied thousands of common variety garden pea plants developed over many generations. Mendel chose pea plants because they grow rapidly, their flowers contain both male and female reproductive organs, and their powderlike pollen can be used to fertilize themselves or cross-pollinate with other plants. Biologist Dawn A. Tamarkin provides a clear explanation of how Mendel worked:

> Mendel figured out that if a pea plant flower was left alone, the male reproductive part (the *anther*) would fertilize the female reproductive part (the *carpel*). The anthers contain pollen, which is actually just a package of sperm. People normally think of sperm as swimming cells, but plants are not in water and have to send their sperm through air. So plants package their sperm into pollen. When the pollen lands on the stigma of the carpel, the sperm within the pollen fertilize the eggs within the *ovules* at the base of the stamen. This fertilization is what leads to a new pea plant seed which will grow into a new pea plant organism.[2]

Mendel first allowed pea plants to self-pollinate, producing offspring that had traits like the parent plants, known as pure-bred plants. He observed seven different characteristics in the plants: short or long stems, purple or white flowers, two different positions of the flowers on the stems, yellow or green pods, yellow or green seeds in the pods, round or wrinkled shape of the seeds, slender or plump shape of the pods.

Mendel began to wonder: What if two pure plants were crossbred? What would happen if a tall plant and a short plant mated, for example? To find out, he took the pollen from the first generation of parent plants (called P1) with short stems and dusted the pollen over P1 plants with long stems. The offspring or next generation of plants, called F1, were tall, which Mendel considered dominant traits. When he crossed the F1 generation, mostly tall plants were produced in the F2 generation, but some short ones appeared also. He analyzed the plants and determined mathematically that although the short plants skipped a generation, their traits (which he called recessive) emerged in the F2 and succeeding generations in a ratio of 3:1.

He also cross-pollinated plants with each of the other contrasting characteristics and kept a careful record of the results. He found that in the first generation, called a hybrid offspring, one of the two traits always appeared, while the other receded until the next generation.

After thousands of these crossbreedings, Mendel concluded that individual characteristics are determined by inherited factors (now called genes). An individual inherits a factor from each parent, but the factors do not combine, as scientists of the time mistakenly theorized. Each factor is passed on intact, but one can be dominant over another.

Although Mendel presented the conclusions from his experiments to the scientific community, no one at the time understood the significance of his findings. Mendel died in 1884, and it was not until the 1900s that the importance of his work was recognized. He laid the foundation for under-standing heredity; later he became known as the "father of modern genetics."

Hybrid Crops

Mendel's work was widely accepted during the early part of the 1900s, but many farmers in the United States still used the conventional method of selecting the best seeds of corn, wheat, oats, or other grains at harvest, and saving them to plant for next year's crop. It was not until the 1930s that crossbreeding plants to create hybrids became common in the United States. When scientists began crossing different pure lines of plants, they found that the first offspring were usually stronger and produced higher yields than their parents. This discovery became known as "hybrid vigor."

Hybrid corn seeds were the first to be marketed broadly across the United States, particularly in Corn Belt states such as Ohio, Indiana, Illinois, and Nebraska. A Nebraska plant scientist and son of a 1930s farmer noted: "In the period of about 10 years . . . this country went from essentially very little hybrid corn to nearly 100 percent. . . . That was a very remarkable, remarkable revolution in agriculture."[3]

However, the "remarkable revolution" had its downside. Hybrid seeds cannot be saved because they do not breed true— that is, they do not consistently produce plants that are like the parents. With hybrid plants, two or more different varieties are cross-pollinated to create offspring that produce a seed variety with characteristics from both of its parents. The seeds that result produce certain characteristics only in the first generation, such as higher yields, a more uniform size, and other desirable traits. But the seed

An archaeological team working in the Euphrates region of Syria found that cultivation of cereal crops actually began around thirteen thousand years ago.

produced by the first generation of the hybrids often reverts to an earlier ancestry and loses much of its yield potential. So farmers must purchase new seed each planting season. As a result, a new hybrid seed industry developed, and by the 1970s, farmers bought seed from companies such as Hi-Bred Corn Company, founded by plant breeder Henry A. Wallace. His company eventually became Pioneer Hi-Bred International, the largest seed company in the United States; it was purchased by DuPont in 1999.

As farmers planted the hybrid corn seeds, they developed millions of acres of one crop. That spelled danger for the corn crop in 1970, when a leaf blight hit and destroyed 15 percent of the U.S. corn crop.[4] Corn plants had become so much alike that they were all at risk for the same diseases and pests.

Such problems led to the use of more pesticides and the development of huge agribusinesses—large multinational corporations that manufacture a variety of agriculture products,

This display of seeds from the 1890s shows the types of crops grown in North Dakota during that time. Hybrid seeds did not come into widespread use in the United States until the 1930s.

from chemical fertilizers to insecticides. Today's agribusinesses control much of the world's food production and are the targets for many critics of biotechnology and GE foods.

Improving Livestock

Before genetic engineering became common practice, livestock breeding to improve food animals was a process of trial and error. For example, farmers selected bulls and cows with desirable traits and mated them to produce cattle with such traits as the ability to resist disease, adapt to harsh weather conditions, and gain weight rapidly (for quick sales).

By the 1940s, American cattle producers were using artificial insemination techniques to breed their livestock. They collected sperm and froze it until they could impregnate cows, which was a more economical method than mating actual cows and bulls. The frozen sperm could be sent to a specific location and was often used to impregnate more than one cow. Artificial insemination also allows breeders to select sperm from bulls with special traits that can be passed on, such as thick skins that resist insects and the ability to adapt to harsh weather conditions. Breeders also use artificial insemination to improve their hogs, horses, and poultry.

New drugs developed in the 1940s and 1950s also brought improvements in livestock production. Streptomycin, for example, helped eradicate tuberculosis in cows and an infection called mastitis in the udders of dairy cattle. Antibiotics were added to animal and chicken feed, as were vitamins, minerals, and other nutrients, which resulted in healthier herds and flocks. However, the overuse of antibiotics in animals, including humans, can result in bacteria that are resistant to drugs. Some critics say that instead of cleaning up unsanitary conditions in industrial agriculture, which would help prevent disease, livestock producers feed an excess of antibiotics to farm animals to keep them healthy, and also use the drugs to promote growth.

Altered Food

Whatever the scientific developments to increase production of crops and food animals, there is little doubt that most of the food for human consumption has been modified in some way for a long time. Currently, many varieties of fruits, vegetables, and even animals produced are not the same as those available four to five decades ago.

In addition, processing industries have changed the foods we eat. If you look at the packaged food items on supermarket shelves, you will see that their labels include information about vitamins, minerals, preservatives, and other ingredients added to the contents. The labels may emphasize antioxidants—vitamins E, C, and beta-carotene (which converts to vitamin A)—because research shows that antioxidants help prevent some diseases, although studies to determine the effects on heart disease and cancer are not conclusive.

An increasing number of unprocessed and processed food products bear an organic label, which means that the ingredients were grown without synthetic fertilizers or pesticides. However, organic foods likely have undergone changes—modified by selective breeding or other processes.

Regardless of all the ways of modifying food that have developed over the years, they are not the same as the modifications that occur with genetic engineering. Those processes take place in the laboratories of universities, foundations, and agribusinesses. The GE seeds that are developed in the labs are planted in agricultural fields, take root, and produce the crops that are part of the ingredients in many of the foods that you eat.

Production of GE Food

If you travel through a rural area in any country where GE crops are grown, you would not know whether corn, soybeans, squash, rapeseed, or other plants are genetically modified. GE plants look just like conventional crops, although in some cases there may be signs alongside the road indicating that GE crops are growing in a nearby fenced field.

Each year since 2003, U.S. farmers have planted more than 320 million acres in major crops, which include corn, sorghum, oats, barley, wheat, rice, soybeans, peanuts, sunflower, cotton, beans, potatoes, sugar beets, canola, and sugarcane, according to the USDA's Economic Research Service (ERS).[1] Of this,

117.6 million acres were planted in GE crops in 2004, making the United States the top country for GE agricultural production. Other countries leading in GE crop production are Canada, Argentina, Brazil, China, and South Africa. GE crops are also grown in such countries as Paraguay, Mexico, Spain, the Philippines, Uruguay, Australia, and Romania.[2]

According to ERS, the most widely adopted GE crops are soybeans and cotton genetically engineered with herbicide-tolerant traits (HT crops), followed by insect-resistant (Bt) cotton and corn. Some of these crops are both insect resistant and herbicide tolerant. The ERS reported that 8 percent of U.S. corn acreage was Bt corn in 1997 then jumped to 26 percent in 1999, rose to 29 percent in 2003 and 35 percent in 2005. Bt cotton plantings increased from 15 percent of U.S. cotton grown in 1997 to 52 percent in 2005.[3]

Worldwide, 8.25 million farmers in seventeen countries planted GE crops in 2004, which was 1.25 million more farmers than did so the previous year. A total of 200 million acres worldwide were planted in GE crops in 2004, according to the International Service for the Acquisition of Agri-biotech Applications (ISAAA). By the end of the decade, ISAAA predicts that up to 15 million farmers will grow GE crops on 370.5 million acres in up to thirty countries.[4]

The GE crops planted are primarily those resistant to herbicides and insects. In the United States, the GE food crops include corn, cotton, soybeans, canola, squash, and a virus-resistant papaya. Other GE crops, such as sugar beets and potatoes, are available in the United States, but they "have yet to be widely adopted by farmers," notes the Pew Initiative on Food and Biotechnology.[5]

Who Are the Producers?

While farmers certainly are food producers, the sources for their GE crop seeds are multinational corporations, often called agricultural-biotechnology (agbiotech) corporations. These huge agbiotech companies produce not only GE seeds but also such agricultural products as insecticides and herbicides.

Since the 1980s, agbiotech firms have been consolidating, buying out and merging with dozens of small chemical and seed companies and pharmaceutical firms. Today, there are "six major agbiotech companies—BASF, Bayer, Dow, DuPont, Monsanto, and Syngenta," and they "have achieved a virtual monopoly" on GE products, according to Henry I. Miller of the Hoover Institution and Gregory Conko of the Competitive Enterprise Institute.[6] By combining both GE seed production and manufacture of chemical pesticides, these huge corporations can develop the pesticides that GE plants (grown from their seed) will resist. Here is how it works in a simple, imaginary scenario:

In 2004, 117.6 million acres were planted in GE crops, making the United States the top country for GE agricultural production.

Suppose you want to have a vegetable garden, and in one part of it you plant green beans, using seeds produced by a major company—call it Amber. Your single plot of ground for the beans, though, is full of pesky weeds that could overpower your plants. So you spray that plot with an herbicide produced by Amber. Your Amber seeds, in this make-believe story, have been engineered to tolerate a specific herbicide, so you do not have to worry that your bean plants will die along with the weeds.

During another season, you plant Amber beans but use an herbicide made by another company, Bombast. Too bad. Your bean plants could fizzle and die because Amber's seeds were not designed to resist Bombast's weed killer. So if you plant Amber seeds, you have to use Amber herbicide or do the sweat labor— pull out the weeds by hand or hack them out with a hoe. The bottom line is that Amber reaps the profits from both its GE seeds and the weed killer you bought.

In the real world, only a few varieties of vegetables and fruits grown in family gardens are genetically modified. But the scenario just described applies to such widely produced commercial crops as corn, soybeans, and canola. Consider the soybeans engineered by the leading biotech company, Monsanto, which claims on its Web site that its GE products "have set the standard by which all others are measured."[7] The company makes huge profits from its Roundup Ready (RR) soybeans that withstand the popular herbicide glyphosate, which Monsanto sells as Roundup. The RR soybeans are genetically modified so that farmers can apply Monsanto's herbicide directly to their fields. Farmers put their seeds in the soil, control the weeds with the herbicide, and as the plants grow, farmers do not have to cultivate fields to destroy weeds. They depend on herbicides to do the job, which saves them time and labor compared to conventional cultivation for weed control. However, the University of Nebraska Agricultural Research Department reported a minor trade-off. Their two-year study showed that "Roundup Ready soybeans yield 6 percent less than their closest conventional relatives and 11 percent less than high-yielding conventional varieties."[8]

Originally, Monsanto began in 1901 as a manufacturer of the artificial sweetener saccharin, but in the 1940s it began producing agricultural chemicals. In the 1960s, the company introduced several herbicides, and the weed killer Roundup went on the market in 1976. By the 1980s, the company was experimenting with genetically modified plants and had also bought a company that produced soybean seeds. Since the mid-1990s, Monsanto has bought out several companies that produce GE seeds, and by 2003, had sold licenses for GE seed production to more than three hundred companies. A licensing agreement allows companies or universities to use Roundup Ready technology to develop soybean varieties best suited for an area's climate and environment.

Canola, also called rapeseed, is used to make oil. Much of the canola grown in the United States is genetically engineered.

A licensing agreement is necessary when a company has a patent on seeds. A patent is a government-issued right to own and control an invention. Seeds and plants, of course, are natural, living products, but when new varieties are developed, they are now often considered "inventions" just as much as a new kind of video game or other mechanism. For example, a Prairie Fire (PVP) hot pepper is a new variety, although not genetically engineered, and its PVP label means Plant Variety Patent; you can plant it and save the seeds for your own use, but you are legally prohibited from selling the seeds.[9]

After the discovery of DNA manipulation, agbiotech companies began to patent GE seeds, plants, bacteria, and animals. They are considered the intellectual property of companies that develop them, and are protected under U.S. and international law. Companies contend that they need the legal protection because of the billions of dollars and years of research spent to develop the technology used to produce genetically modified organisms with valuable traits. In the case of GE patented seeds, unlike the hot pepper variety seeds, farmers and gardeners legally cannot save seeds and replant them the following season.

Patent Violations

For thousands of years, farmers worldwide have saved their best seeds—corn, wheat, rice, or whatever—for replanting, and that practice continues for a variety of non-GE plants harvested in numerous countries. But major agricultural firms such as Dow, DuPont, Monsanto, and Syngenta are demanding greater control over the GE seeds they create, and these corporations use a variety of testing methods to detect use of their GE technologies. For example, farmers who buy Roundup Ready soybeans do not have the option of replanting any leftover seed or those saved from harvests. They must sign a technology agreement that says they are buying the seed "solely to produce a single commercial crop in one and only one season."[10] They cannot sell any leftover soybeans to anyone for planting—farmers must buy new GE seed each season.

The Monsanto agreement also stipulates that the company can send their officials to inspect fields for several consecutive years to determine whether farmers are "technology pirates," illegally planting GE seed, which by law is stealing technology. In fact, the major seed companies spend tens of millions of dollars each year to check up on farmers suspected of replanting. Companies argue that they are justified in going after violators in order to recover costs for research and development; in the case of Monsanto those costs totaled $145 million in 2004 alone.[11]

According to the Center for Food Safety (CFS), an advocacy organization working for regulation of GE crops, Monsanto "aggressively" investigates farmers it suspects of violating agreements and pressures farmers "to settle out of court for an undisclosed sum." Others have been sued. As of 2005, the company had filed ninety lawsuits against farmers.[12]

Law professor Drew L. Kershen of Vermont, who studied the CFS report, noted that Monsanto has won seventy-three of the ninety cases, "with a number of legal wins coming in front of a jury." In addition, Kershen wrote that he found from published judicial opinions about the lawsuits that "all the farmers, except one, have admitted that they intentionally acquired Monsanto patented seed without signing a license agreement or that they purposefully saved Monsanto patented seed in violation of the signed technology use agreement prohibiting the saving of seed for replanting in the following year."[13]

One South Carolina farmer, Carlyle Price, learned the hard way that saving GE seed is not a smart thing to do. Price, in partnership with his brother and cousins, grows 7,500 acres of crops. In 2003, he planted Roundup Ready soybeans saved from the 2000 and 2001 plantings. At the time, he had not signed a contract with Monsanto, owner of the RR patent, and thought he "might have to pay a small fee later." He told a reporter that he got the impression from seed dealers that planting the seed "wasn't as serious as it turned out to be."[14]

Nine officials from Monsanto investigated the Price farm, and after eight months the company and Price settled out of court. Price paid $1.5 million in royalty fees to Monsanto. He also agreed to spread the word about his experience among other farmers. For the record, Price said "I now realize that the intellectual property rights of seed companies have to be protected. I think if I had known this [earlier], I would have never saved Roundup Ready seed."[15]

Another more complex and lengthy conflict with Monsanto occurred in Canada, where Percy Schmeiser and his wife have been farming in Saskatoon, Saskatchewan, since 1947, producing rapeseed for canola on 1,000 acres. The Schmeisers had long saved their canola seeds to improve their production. In 1988, Monsanto sued Schmeiser had obtained the seed without a license. "Up to that time I never had anything to do with Monsanto's GE canola. I'd never bought their seed or gone to a Monsanto meeting. I didn't even know a Monsanto rep," Percy Schmeiser declares on a Web site he established to fight genetically altered food.[16]

According to numerous news reports about his predicament, Schmeiser in 1997 sprayed Roundup to kill weeds growing along the edge of one of his fields, and accidentally discovered rapeseed plants that resisted Roundup. Other Canadian farmers had planted Roundup Ready canola varieties the year before, and Schmeiser maintained that rapeseeds had blown onto his property from nearby farms. After he sprayed Roundup on his canola field, he found that many of the plants survived. That year, as he had always done, he saved his seeds for planting in 1998.

Apparently neighbors reported to Monsanto that they suspected Schmeiser was growing Roundup Ready canola. Monsanto inspectors, mill operators, and the court tested samples taken from all of Schmeiser's fields, and tests "revealed that 95 to 99% of Schmeiser's 1998 crop was genetically engineered," according to a report by a Cornell University's Cooperative Extension.[17]

In 2001, a federal judge found Schmeiser guilty of violating the patent law. The judge ruled that in 1998 Schmeiser planted seed saved from 1997, "which he knew or ought to have known was Roundup tolerant."[18] Schmeiser appealed and lost again in 2002. His case finally went to the Canadian Supreme Court, which in 2004 agreed with lower court rulings that Schmeiser had infringed the patent law. But he was not required to pay penalties to Monsanto—profits from his 1998 crop, damages, court costs, or the technology use fee of $15 per acre.

Schmeiser expressed mixed emotions about the ruling. He was disappointed that the Court found the patent law valid, which means that only Parliament in Canada (and Congress in the United States) can determine whether a company's patent has priority over farmers' long-held practice of saving and reusing their seeds. But Schmeiser believes that the High Court's ruling will make it difficult for Monsanto to sue other farmers for patent infringement:

> They are now going to have to prove that a farmer profited from having RR canola in their field. The Court noted that my profits were the same whether I had conventional canola or RR canola, so I find it hard to see how Monsanto can say in any future case that the farmer made more money because of their product. This decision may have removed the 'teeth' from their patent.[19]

Detecting GMOs

Of course Monsanto is not the only one of the major agribusinesses that holds patents or seeks to protect its GMOs.

This soy farmer in Mississippi was charged by Monsanto for saving seed from one harvest to plant the next year, a practice that goes against the company's patent agreement.

Firms such as Dow, DuPont, and Syngenta are also demanding greater control over the GE seeds they create, and these corporations use a variety of testing methods to detect use of their GE technologies. To avoid patent violations—as well as to guarantee that they are selling non-GE crops—testing is also important to farmers, grain elevator operators, and seed merchants. Also concerned are individuals and organizations opposed to GE foods.

One common test can be conducted with a few simple tools included in a purchased kit. First, you would crush a seed or use a small piece of leaf or stem sample from a plant, mix it with water, then dip a testing strip from the kit into this mixture. The strip changes color to indicate whether a GMO is present. Within five to twenty minutes you could have a result.

More complex tests take place in a laboratory and require highly skilled technicians. Lab personnel commonly apply a technology that can detect low concentrations of specific genes in a GE crop or processed food. It may take three to five days or even weeks to determine the results.

No matter how sophisticated, tests are limited and no test today can determine that a crop or product is totally free of GMOs. That worries people who are opposed to GE food crops, and it is just one of many issues that critics address.

4 **Opposing and Protesting
GE Products**

Monster Crops, Mutant Meals, Suicide Seeds, Frankenfoods—
these terms are meant to label GE products as some type of
concoction developed by scientists gone berserk. The
Frankenfoods label, which is used most often in news articles,
refers to a subhuman character in a novel by British author
Mary Shelley. Published in 1818, the story is about a brilliant
scientist, Dr. Frankenstein, who creates a monster that eventually turns on him. The story was also hugely popular in stage
and movie adaptations.

When opponents of GE products use the Frankenfood term,
they imply that science has created unnatural and possibly

dangerous foods. While processed foods such as breakfast cereals and frozen meals with GE components do not appear to be hazardous to human health, critics say there is no certainty that is true. Genetic engineering could pose risks that scientists simply are unable to identify at this time, opponents claim.

Where Are the Critics?

Despite the fact that millions of farmers produce GE food crops in many countries, opponents of GMOs can be found around the world. European nations, for example, have resisted GE crops since they became an issue in 1996. In 1998, the European Union (EU), which includes Great Britain, Germany, France, Greece, and twenty-one other countries, banned the import of GE crops, but in 2004 permitted the import of clearly labeled GE maize (corn) that resists insects and herbicides. In 2005, the EU permitted the import of GE rapeseed.

The EU decision prompted much criticism from opponents who question the safety of GE corn over the long term.[1] One of the concerns is about "markers." When a foreign gene is spliced into a plant, it is often linked to another gene known as a marker. This helps scientists determine whether the splicing process has been successful. But some people fear the use of antibiotic-resistant markers, which they say could reduce the effectiveness of antibiotics to fight human diseases. One company, Syngenta, declares its antibiotic-resistant marker genes are safe but will follow national regulations to use other markers when they become available.

Even in nations considered GE friendly, such as the United States and Canada, concerns about GE food have been widely publicized in the news media since the late 1990s. That is due in part to activities of such environmental groups as Biodemocracy, Bioengineering Action Network, EarthSave, Friends of the Earth, Greenpeace, Say No to GMOs, Sierra Club, True Foods mpaign, and others, as well as some grassroots groups from around the world.

Protests have occurred in numerous countries with activists pulling up GE plants or running over fields with GE crops to destroy them. Activists have also staged demonstrations before meetings of the Biotechnology Industry Organization (BIO), the world's largest convention of biotech and pharmaceutical executives, and the World Trade Organization (WTO). Critics are upset with WTO because it lodged a complaint brought by the United States, Canada, and Argentina against the European Union's moratorium on GE crops.

Global Protests

GE critics around the world protest because they believe they have legitimate concerns. Many opponents of GMOs contend that there are questions about morality and ethics in the industrialization of agriculture. Some point to the fact that only a handful of agbiotech companies from wealthy nations are trying to determine food production in developing countries, making those nations dependent on these corporations for their agricultural supplies.

Others argue that huge agbiotech firms are misleading the public by claiming that GE crops will increase the world's food supply and feed the hungry in poor nations. An activist protesting during a BIO meeting in San Francisco insisted: "Hunger is not caused by a deficit of food production. It is a deficit of morality. It is a deficit of distribution."[2] Indeed, some economists say poor people may starve because they cannot afford the food that is available or because they have no access to food that is controlled by dictators, bandits, or rebels at war.

Christian Aid, a coalition of churches in Great Britain and Ireland, has frequently pointed out that increasing food production is not necessarily an answer to hunger and famine. Rather, contributing factors include "large gaps between rich and poor, ownership of resources concentrated in too few hands, and a food supply based on too few varieties of crops."[3]

In a report called *Selling Suicide* published in 1999, Christian Aid acknowledged that genetic engineering could possibly benefit poor people and poor farmers, but only if certain conditions were taken into account, such as whether GE crops can be part of existing farming practices; whether land is available to grow diverse crops, not just GE varieties; and whether GE crops will have an adverse impact on those already being grown.[4]

> **Opponents of genetic engineering claim that GE foods could pose risks that scientists simply are unable to identify at this time.**

Debates Over Terminator Seeds

In the early 1990s, the USDA, in cooperation with a Texas seed company, developed what technically is known as genetic use restriction technologies (GURT) but is more commonly called terminator technology. It involves several genes that in a complex system within a plant can make its seeds sterile—they will not reproduce. The technology was created to protect corporation patents and to prevent farmers from saving GE seeds and replanting them; they must buy new seeds each season. GURT also prevents GE crops from contaminating conventionally grown plants and eliminates the need to segregate GE crops from non-GE crops. But the terminator patent is quite broad and applies to both GE seeds and those bred by conventional means, which would give major seed companies control over much of the commercial seed market. In addition, terminator technology could have a detrimental effect on millions of poor farmers around the world who cannot afford to buy seed each year. Their main seed source is their farm-saved seeds and those they exchange with their neighbors.

In 1999, Monsanto gave up its plan to commercialize terminator seeds, which by then were being called "suicide seeds" and "demon seeds" in opponents' messages. Since 1999, there has been a worldwide moratorium on the use of terminator technology. Nevertheless, the campaign against GURTs continues, because several biotech companies are seeking new patents on the technology, and some companies along with the USDA are advocating in favor of terminator technology. In addition, the Canadian government is attempting to overturn the international moratorium, according to the group formerly known as RAFI (now called ETC, the Action Group on Erosion, Technology and Concentration). According to ETC's director Pat Mooney, this is "a devastating kick in the stomach to the world's most vulnerable farmers."[5]

Environmental Concerns

Many critics of GE crops are groups and individuals troubled about the environment, and they have voiced their complaints for years. For example, some environmentalists express concern that farmers who plant herbicide-tolerant crops will use more herbicides than necessary to control weeds and will destroy natural food sources for birds and some animals. Other concerns include possible harmful effects on nontarget organisms when toxin is released into the soil from roots of Bt crops. According to the Union of Concerned Scientists (UCS), "it is unlikely all potential harms to the environment have been identified," and projecting what might go wrong "depends on how well scientists understand the organism and the environment into which it is released. At this point, biology and ecology are too poorly understood to be certain that question has been answered comprehensively."[6]

Other questions have yet to be answered: Who will be responsible if there are harmful effects of GMOs? What can farmers do if GE crops appear accidentally in their fields? The latter question concerns many organic farmers and consumers. In the United States, standards set by the USDA require that

A geneticist transfers selected alfalfa DNA clones as part of the process of making genetic markers. Some people worry about the problems that they say adding marker genes could cause.

growers of certified organic food cannot intentionally use GE seeds, and food must be free of irradiation and grown without artificial pesticides and fertilizers. Animals raised for organic food must be free of antibiotics, growth promoters, or other drugs. Maintaining these standards has become increasingly difficult as GE crops and animal feed have proliferated in the world's food supply, threatening to contaminate organic foods.

GE Contamination

In the context of genetically modified crops, contamination means the spread of GE traits to non-GE plants. If, for example, weed relatives of GE plants are growing near a field of GE crops, pollen from the modified plants can transfer traits to the weeds, allowing them to flourish and become "superweeds." This means that weed management becomes more difficult, and farmers are likely to use more chemicals to control them.

A report by the U.S. National Academy of Sciences, *Biological Confinement of Genetically Engineered Organisms and Nature Biotechnology*, points out that preventing contamination of non-GE crops or wild relatives has not been possible in many cases. Why? Because nature intrudes.

As with weed relatives of GE plants, cross-pollination (or gene flow, as it is often called) occurs when pollen is carried by the wind or by insects to non-GE crops. In the United States, buffer zones—vacant or weed-filled plots—are supposed to surround fields where GE crops are grown, keeping them a specified distance from conventional crops. But in some cases, seed companies plant test fields of GE corn or soybeans too close to nonmodified plants, causing contamination.

Contamination can also occur after harvest. GE seeds, or parts of root crops like sugar beets that have been modified, may stay in a field and sprout the next season. Stray GE seeds may spill during transport to mills or from farm equipment onto non-GE fields. In addition, some modified seed varieties get mixed up with conventional seeds.

No matter how it takes place, GE contamination has been reported in more than sixty countries, and in June 2005, GeneWatch UK and Greenpeace International launched the first online register of GE contamination incidents. The Internet site was initiated because "no Government or international agency has yet established a public record of contamination incidents or of other problems associated with [GE] crops," said Dr. Sue Mayer, GeneWatch director in Britain.[7]

Debate Over Mexican Maize

Much controversy has surrounded reports of maize (corn) contamination in Mexico. In November 2001, the scientific journal *Nature* published a study by two scientists from the University of California at Berkeley, Ignacio Chapela and David Quist, who concluded after testing native maize from isolated mountain areas of Oaxaca, Mexico, that it was contaminated with corn genetically modified with the soil bacterium *Bacillus thuringiensis* (Bt). Bt is a toxin that kills pests such as the corn borer.

The *Nature* article raised alarms worldwide because the contamination of Mexican corn occurred in the area where maize was domesticated thousands of years ago. The Mexican government had banned any planting of GE corn in 1998 to protect its native varieties of corn. Yet it appeared that GE corn had been planted by Mexican farmers who had purchased seed imported from the United States, not knowing that it was a modified variety.

Some scientists highly criticized the *Nature* article, including several from Berkeley. One critic claimed that the study by Chapela and Quist was "a testament to technical incompetence"and that the authors had skewed their conclusions to support antibiotech views.[8] On the other side, environmentalists and other activists accused critics of pandering to big corporations that had provided grants to Berkeley for GE crop research.

After much dissent, a *Nature* editorial backed away from the findings of Chapela and Quist, declaring "that the evidence available is not sufficient to justify the publication of the original paper."[9] However, the Mexican government appeared to support Chapela and Quist when the National Ecology Institute at the Mexican environment ministry declared: "Genetic contamination of wild Mexican varieties is taking place. On average, 8 percent of plants showed signs of GM contamination, although in other fields we found more than 10 percent."[10] And the study's authors conceded only minor interpretive errors. "We certainly stand by our original, main statement and I have yet to see anyone challenge it legitimately," said Ignacio Chapela, coauthor of the study with David Quist.[11]

The claims and counterclaims about contaminated Mexican corn went on for the next several years. In the meantime, in 2003 and 2004, researchers from Mexico and the United States gathered more than 153,000 seeds from 870 maize plants in 125 fields in Oaxaca. Researchers sent these seeds to two commercial companies in the United States that test for very low concentrations of transgenic material in maize seeds.

Allison Snow, a biology professor at Ohio State University who helped lead the new study, and other researchers thought that 5 to 10 percent of the corn would be contaminated. "There is great potential for transgenes to come across the U.S. border, with millions of tons of GM grain imported each year for processed food and animal feed," Snow reported.[12] But the researchers were surprised by the findings: There was no evidence of genetically modified corn in the native varieties. The results, however, should not be applied to other regions of Mexico, the study said, because in the future transgenes in Mexican maize could be found elsewhere in the country.[13]

The owner of a cornfield in Oaxaca, Mexico, holds up an ear of GE corn. A study in the journal *Nature* reported that native maize had been contaminated with genetically modified corn.

Bt Corn Issues

Even before the controversy surrounding Mexican corn, a widely publicized issue involving Bt corn arose in 1999 when an article by Cornell entomologist John Losey appeared in *Nature*. Losey reported on laboratory findings that he and colleagues conducted with monarch butterfly larvae (caterpillars) and their preferred food, milkweed plants. In the lab, the researchers dusted the milkweed with pollen from Bt corn, which killed the caterpillars within four days.

After the Cornell paper was published, national and international news coverage prompted controversy worldwide among the agbiotech industry, scientists, farmers, and environmentalists. The colorful monarch butterfly, frequently studied by schoolchildren and nature lovers, became a symbol for GM opponents of what could go wrong with genetically modified crops. As Margaret Mellon of the UCS put it: "Once we heard about the *Nature* paper, we called reporters and sent out press releases for days. We worked very hard to make this a high-profile issue because without media attention we knew nothing would be done."[14] In the view of UCS, the findings illustrated that risk assessment studies for GM foods were superficial at best.

However, in 2000 a major research effort got under way with a team of Canadian and U.S. scientists from universities and governments to determine the impact of Bt on the monarch butterfly. The team submitted papers to *The Proceedings of the National Academy of Sciences (PNAS)*, which were examined by independent reviewers and published in 2001. According to a National Academy of Sciences report:

> In most commercial [corn] hybrids, Bt expression in pollen is low, and laboratory and field studies show no acute toxic effects at any pollen density that would be encountered in the field. . . . This 2-year study suggests that the impact of Bt corn pollen from current commercial hybrids on monarch butterfly populations is negligible.[15]

Yet research conducted in Great Britain over a three-year period demonstrated that GE crops can be harmful to wildlife such as butterflies, bees, and possibly songbirds. The British government commissioned a study of modified spring rapeseed, sugar beets, maize, and winter rapeseed. While field tests of the GE maize showed no harm to wildlife, the other GE crops had a negative impact.

In March 2005, a variety of news sources reported the study's results, which were published in the *Proceedings of the Royal Society of London*.[16] In fields where GE winter rapeseed grew, the number of bees in the fields dropped by half and the number of butterflies by up to two thirds compared to fields with traditional rapeseed.

British researchers concluded that the modified rapeseed, which is engineered to resist a particular herbicide, allows a potent weed killer to be used in fields, killing more broad-leafed weeds than grassy varieties. Bees and butterflies prefer the former type of weed, and songbirds feed on broad-leafed wildflowers. According to one report from the Centre for Ecology and Hydrology in Lancaster, the GE plots had "one-third fewer seeds from broad-leaved flowers" than the "fields with conventional oilseed rape." The lead researcher noted, "These differences were still present two years after the crop had been sown. . . . So we've got a significant biological difference that is carrying on from season to season."[17] Environmentalists contend that the tests in Britain were proof that planting GE crops is harmful to wildlife.

Health Hazards?

GE critics concerned about health hazards believe more scientific investigations should focus on whether GE crops used in foods can cause such problems as cancer, birth defects, or allergies. One human health hazard of GE crops that has gained much attention is the risk of creating a product that causes allergies. That was the focus in 2000 when StarLink corn was found in taco shells and other products made from corn. StarLink was developed with one type of Bt toxin called CRY9C to protect plants from caterpillar pests as well as to make them resistant to some weed killers. The EPA approved the corn itself for animal feed only, not for human consumption, because of the possibility that StarLink could cause allergic reactions in humans. According to a report from Cornell Cooperative Extension:

> After the discovery of StarLink contamination, two dozen people came forward claiming that they had had severe allergic reactions after eating StarLink corn products. Seventeen of the 24 allowed blood samples to be tested by the FDA and the Centers for Disease

Control and Prevention (CDC). The CDC released a report on June 13, 2001, concluding that although the claimants did appear to have had severe allergic reactions to something, blood tests demonstrated that StarLink was not the cause. To date, there have been no documented cases of allergic reactions to StarLink corn.[18]

Nevertheless, manufacturers recalled an estimated three hundred or more corn-based products. In addition, Aventis CropScience, producers of the CRY9C corn, bought up the harvests from the 1999 and 2000 corn crop, paying millions of dollars in compensation to farmers. StarLink corn cannot be sold for human consumption, but it turned up in corn shipped to Japan and South Korea, who were major importers of U.S. corn for food manufacturing. Consequently, the imports of U.S. corn for food processing dropped considerably in these two countries in 2000 and 2001.[19]

Scientists discovered another problem with allergens when they isolated the gene in Brazil nuts that provides nutritional benefits and transferred it to soybeans. After engineering the new soybean plants, testing showed that the modified soybeans could cause reactions in people allergic to Brazil nuts. As a result, there were no further efforts to create GE soybeans with Brazil nut genes.

Health concerns also focus on pharma crops. These are crops modified to produce pharmaceuticals (medicinal drugs), biologics (such as vaccines and blood products), and industrial chemicals. Pharma crops are modified in the same way that GE foods are produced. Using rDNA techniques, scientists isolate genes for pharmaceutical or industrial products and insert these transgenes into corn, tobacco, or other crops. The modified plants then produce drugs, vaccines, or industrial chemicals in their leaves, roots, or seeds.

Most of these modified crops are still in the field-testing stages, but they have elicited much resistance from opponents. In the first place, no one knows the exact effects pharma crops

These protesters in Washington, D.C., claim that Bt corn is toxic to the monarch butterfly. Scientists disagree about the impact of genetically engineered crops on wildlife.

would have on humans. Some of the substances they produce, such as industrial and research chemicals, were never intended for human consumption, and can be harmful if accidentally ingested.

Critics also point out that pharma crops can contaminate nonmodified plants used in processed foods. Indeed, in 2002, USDA officials discovered that modified corn plants with a pharmaceutical protein were growing in soybean fields in Iowa and Nebraska. During the previous season, ProdiGene, a Texas-based company, had used the sites as test plots for drug-producing corn, and leftover seeds sprouted among the soybean plants. The USDA quarantined all the harvested soybeans, ordered that nearby cornfields be burned, and charged

ProdiGene $250,000 to reimburse the agency for cleaning up contamination.

Another company, Ventria Biosciences, encountered fierce opposition to its plan to grow pharma rice. The company at first attempted to test its modified rice in Missouri, but the brewer Anheuser-Busch, which is based in Missouri and uses rice in its processing, and Riceland Foods of Arkansas protested, as did 175 Missouri rice farmers. Anheuser-Busch's vice president told the Associated Press: "Given the potential for contamination of commercial rice production in this state, we will not purchase any rice produced or processed in Missouri if Ventria introduces its pharma rice here."[20]

Ventria and its experimental rice were also rejected in California, where growers feared that their crop would be contaminated and would be banned in Japan, a major importer that restricts GE crops. The company's latest site is in North Carolina, although the Missouri governor has expressed hope that Ventria rice can be grown in his state on sites far from conventional crops. And Anheuser-Busch withdrew its threatened boycott after Ventria promised to plant its pharma rice 120 miles away from Missouri's rice lands.[21]

So does this mean that pharma crops are safe after all? That question is still to be answered as are others about possible risks of GE plants to human health and the environment, the main concern of anti-GE forces. In the meantime, though, there are many GE proponents who firmly believe genetic modification will transform agriculture and people's lives on a global scale.

Reaping the Benefits of GMOs

What if you could swallow a pill with a vaccine made from the leaves or parts of GE vegetables or fruits? Would you opt for that rather than get a shot? What if GE crops could alleviate hunger in many parts of the world? Would you support such an effort? What if you had the expertise to create healthier farm animals with GMOs? Would you apply your knowledge to that end? What if GE seeds could reduce the use of toxic pesticides that pollute the environment? Would you plant those seeds?

As you might expect, advocates of GE foods likely would have positive responses to questions about the types of actions they would take to encourage genetic engineering of plants and animals. Just as opponents speak out against GMOs so do advocates have their say. Supporters frequently tout the benefits of GMOs, speaking through organizations or as individuals.

What They Say

In 2005, the World Health Organization of the United Nations issued a report entitled "Modern Food Biotechnology, Human Health and Development," which concluded that GMOs have the potential to increase crop yield and improve nutritional quality of food. That in turn "can contribute directly to enhancing human health and development." There may also be "indirect benefits such as reduction in agricultural chemical usage" and "enhanced farm income." Though the report stresses the need for continued safety assessments on GMOs before they are marketed, it points out that those GE products already on the international market "have passed risk assessments and are not likely to, nor have [been] shown to, present risks for human health."[1]

Another group supporting GMOs includes more than thirty-four hundred scientists from around the world, among them twenty-five Nobel prize winners, who have signed a Declaration in Support of Agricultural Biotechnology since it was first presented in 2000. The declaration says in part:

> No food products, whether produced with recombinant DNA techniques or with more traditional methods, are totally without risk. The risks posed by foods are a function of the biological characteristics of those foods and the specific genes that have been used, not of the processes employed in their development. Our goal as scientists is to ensure that any new foods produced from recombinant DNA are as safe or safer than foods already being consumed.[2]

An organization called the Council for Biotechnology Information (CBI), which is made up of members of the leading agbiotech companies and trade associations, has published the booklet "Good Ideas Are Growing—Plant Biotechnology" to spread their views regarding the advantages of GE crops. The booklet points out that "A 2002 study of biotech crops by the nonprofit National Center for Food and Agricultural Policy (NCFAP) found that six biotech crops planted in the United States—soybeans, corn, cotton, papaya, squash and canola— produced an additional 4 billion pounds of food and fiber on the same acreage, improved farm income by $1.5 billion and reduced pesticide use by 46 million pounds" than in previous years.[3]

The NCFAP study was supported with grants from the Rockefeller Foundation, the Biotechnology Industry Organization, CropLife America, Council for Biotechnology Information, Grocery Manufacturers of America, and Monsanto. In 2004, NCFAP released another study showing that together the six main biotech crops increased grower income by $1.9 billion in 2003 as well as boosting net yields by 5.3 billion pounds and cutting pesticide use by 46.4 million pounds.[4]

The American Medical Association, the International Society of African Scientists, the Organization for Economic Cooperation and Development, the Food and Agricultural Organization of the United Nations, and Truth about Trade and Technology are other organizations that have voiced their support for GE plants. So have some U.S. farm groups such as the National Corn Growers Association (NCGA), the American Soybean Association (ASA), the National Cotton Council (NCC), and the American Farm Bureau. Leaders of these groups met in Chicago in May 2005 to recognize the planting of the one-billionth acre of GE crops, or what those at the conference called "biotech-enhanced agricultural commodities."

The World Health Organization concluded that GMOs have the potential to increase crop yield and improve nutritional quality of food, thus enhancing human health and development.

"U.S. farmers are adopting biotechnology because they recognize [its] safety, benefits and potential," according to Darrin Ihnen, a South Dakota farmer who heads the NCGA's Biotechnology Working Group. "As a farmer, it's important that I find ways to become more efficient in my operation. Biotechnology helps reduce the amount of insecticides and herbicides I use." ASA's leader Neal Bredehoeft agrees. "Farmers are both producers and consumers of the food and fiber [such as cotton] that comes from our farms," he noted. "This dual position helps us recognize that biotechnology is another in a long line of advancements that have helped make our supply of food and fiber the safest and healthiest in the world."[5]

What do farmers in other parts of the world think about GE crops? The Council for Biotechnology Information has compiled views from farmers representing seven countries besides the United States. Mahalingappa Shankarikoppa, a cotton farmer in India, says, "With biotech cotton, I make two to three times what I used to with the old, traditional seeds. And I spray [insecticides] 80 percent less than I did before." Filipino corn farmer Edwin Paraluman, who planted ten acres of Bt corn, declares, "For me, it's really amazing. This is the first time in my life that I can actually get ahead and provide a better life for my family." T. J. Buthelezi, who raises Bt cotton in South Africa, noted: "For the first time, I'm making money. I can pay my debts." Lucian Buzdugan, a Romanian soybean farm manager, says he is "grateful that I now have the training to grow biotech soybeans." He has seen his income and yields double by planting GE soybeans on the twenty-three farms he manages near the Black Sea about 175 miles east of Bucharest.[6]

GE Crop Benefits

After Bt crops—corn, cotton, and potatoes—became commercially available in 1996, scientists around the globe began studying the effects of these biotech plants. Over

A plant physiologist compares two types of genetically engineered tomatoes. Supporters of biotech agriculture say it will result in more crops at lower expense and with less use of chemical pesticides.

a decade, researchers found that insects did not build up a resistance to Bt crops. This far surpassed the time period when insects begin to resist most conventional pesticides.[7]

Farmers worldwide who have planted GE crops point out that engineered plants with the Bt toxin have been an economic boon. Growers have been able to reduce costly pesticide use and increase yields and income with GE crops, according to reports from such organizations as the Council for Agricultural Science and Technology, National Center for Food and Agricultural Policy, the U.S. Department of Agriculture, the Environmental Protection Agency, and others.

Studies of Bt cotton have shown increased benefits for farmers in two very different locations: small farm plots in India and commercial cotton fields in Arizona. In India, analysts found Bt crop yields up 80 percent compared to neighbors' farms where conventional cotton was grown. Scientists analyzed Arizona data from 1991 to 1995 regarding pink bollworm, a pest found in nearly all cotton fields worldwide. The pink bollworm lays its eggs on cotton bolls. When the eggs hatch, the larvae eat the cottonseeds, causing millions of dollars of damage to the fiber. After Bt cotton was introduced, bollworm populations dropped, and more than 60 percent of the cotton acreage was free of the pest.[8]

Environmental Protections

Along with better pest control, GE crops help protect the environment because there is less runoff of synthetic pesticides as well as herbicides into groundwater and streams. A study by the nonprofit Conservation Technology Information Center at Purdue University found that with herbicide-tolerant crops farmers could institute conservation tillage—low or no cultivation of soil to get rid of weeds. Plowing was once the primary method to destroy weeds and to prepare a field for planting. But such cultivation also led to soil erosion and destroyed wildlife food sources. With herbicide tolerant plants and conservation tillage, soil erosion has been reduced by one billion tons each year. One Iowa farmer who switched to conservation tillage in the 1990s said he lost less soil on his farm in ten years than he did in one year with conventional plowing.

Another benefit of conservation tillage is plant residue. Plant material is allowed to lay on the surface and hold moisture in the soil, which prevents runoff of sediment into streams and protects the habitat of fish and other aquatic life.

One more environmental protection occurs with conservation tillage: Farmers do not have to make as many passes through their fields to plow as they would with conventional cultivation. This not only saves them more than 309 million gallons of fuel each year, according to the study, but it also reduces carbon dioxide, one of the greenhouse gases contributing to warming the earth.[9]

Helping Poor Farmers

GE crop advocates often say that biotech crops can help feed hungry populations around the world and provide food security—that is, assure a long-term, safe, and adequate food supply. Although there are food surpluses in some areas, food production will need to increase threefold in order to feed an estimated 3 billion more people expected to populate the earth in fifty years, some experts say. Currently 800 million people worldwide are "chronically malnourished, and 3 billion struggle to survive on less than $700 a year," according to leaders of the Congress of Racial Equality (CORE).[10] CORE is a U.S. civil rights organization whose national chairman Roy Innis points out, "Over 70% of Africans are employed in farming full time. Yet, half of [African] countries rely on emergency food aid. Within ten years, Africa will be home to three-fourths of the world's hungry people."[11]

Paul Driessen, CORE's senior policy adviser, criticizes environmental groups for stifling economic development in the third world by, among other things, standing in the way of GE crops that would benefit poor farmers. In an article on the topic, Driessen writes:

> Many of [Africa's] farmers are women who labor sunup to sundown on 3 to 5 acre plats. They rarely have enough crops to feed their own families, much less sell for extra money. Millions live on less than a dollar a day. Maize [corn] is southern Africa's most important crop. But because of drought, insects, poor soil, plant diseases and lack of technology, the average yield per acre is the lowest in the world. Other crops suffer similar fates.[12]

To underscore GE crop benefits, the article tells about a South African woman who grows GE maize. She says that she saw her

> old plants . . . destroyed by insects, but not the new biotech plants. With the profits I get from the new Bt maize, I can grow onions, spinach and tomatoes, and sell them for extra money to buy fertilizer. We were struggling to keep hunger out of our houses. Now the future looks good. If someone came and said we should stop using the new maize, I would cry.[13]

Africa

In early 2005, CORE held a biotechnology conference at the United Nations, and during the gathering, directors presented a video in which African farmers described how GE crops have improved their lives. The video, *Voices from Africa: Biotechnology and the Subsistence Farmer*, includes interviews with African scientists who help convey the message that "Africa needs a new agricultural revolution," as CORE leader Roy Innis puts it. He adds that a biotechnology revolution is "not a magic bullet. But it is a vital weapon in Africa's thus far losing struggle against malnutrition, poverty, despair and deepening anger."[14]

Farmers in Zambia weed a maize field. Zambia has rejected the offer of GE food as aid.

Indeed, a *Christian Science Monitor* story points out that 31.1 million Africans, "scattered across Sudan's Darfur region, Zimbabwe, Ethiopia, Uganda, and elsewhere" are food deprived. "Despite progress in boosting democracy, ending wars, and economic growth, Africa is the only region in the world becoming less and less able to feed itself." There are numerous reasons for the problem, such as drought, the spread of desert land, increased population, inefficient governments, and poor roads and transportation to get food aid and local crops to places where they are needed.[15]

Another voice urging that Africa take advantage of GE crops to help relieve hunger and poverty is the International

Food Policy Research Institute (IFPRI). The institute receives funds from sixty-four governments, private foundations, and international and regional organizations known as the Consultative Group on International Agricultural Research. In mid-2005, the IFPRI released a study on public institutions in four countries—Egypt, Kenya, South Africa, and Zimbabwe—that are conducting research to produce GE crops. Joel Cohen, IFPRI Senior Research Fellow and an author of the study, says that "Corporations are often seen as the only drivers of GE foods, but the reality is that a few African countries, despite their limited financial and technical resources, have vibrant public biotech research programs."[16]

According to the study, current biotech research has the potential to reduce the use of pesticides, increase drought tolerance, and improve the nutritional value of staple foods. These changes could benefit the environment, improve health, reduce the cost of food, and increase the incomes of poor smallholder farmers throughout Africa.

The research focuses on twenty different crops, including maize, sweet potato, and cowpeas, to improve their resistance to diseases and pests that can devastate yields for African farmers. However, most of the public research is still in laboratory, greenhouse, or confined field trials. "Most African countries, like many other poor countries, often cannot advance GE crop research because their national policies or regulatory systems are not prepared to deal with safety requirements for approving general use," Cohen explained. "As poor countries develop stronger biosafety procedures, they will be increasingly able to manage potential risks associated with GE crops."[17]

Outside Africa

From other parts of the world come reports that GE crops are providing economic and health benefits for small farmers. In China, for example, "surveys of randomly selected farm households that are cultivating the insect-resistant GE rice varieties demonstrate that when compared with households cultivating non-GE rice, small and poor farm households benefit from adopting GE rice," according to researchers in China and at Rutgers University and the University of California, Davis. The surveys found that yields from one of the GE varieties "were 9 percent higher than those of conventional rice varieties." GE rice also brought savings in the quantity and costs of pesticides, which were eight to ten times less for insect-resistant rice than for conventional rice.[18]

Researchers also investigated whether reduced use of pesticides resulted in fewer health problems. (Illness due to pesticides is common in many developing countries.) The result? "None of the farmers who had completely planted their farms to genetically modified insect-resistant rice varieties reported experiencing adverse health effects from pesticide use in either 2002 or 2003," according to the survey. In contrast, investigators found that among farmers who planted conventional rice and used pesticides, 8.3 percent of the farm households in 2002 and 3 percent in 2003 reported health problems.[19]

Support for Pharma Crops

American agriculture has helped feed the world, and "now we want to improve the world's health with it," says Scott Deeter, head of Ventria Biosciences, the company that was at first prevented from planting pharma rice in Missouri. But in 2005, it was able to move to the state where it will cultivate rice containing human genes. The modified rice can make proteins that would be used to create medicines for stomach disorders.

Not too many years ago, scientists thought that they could develop "edible vaccines"—drugs that could be taken by eating raw plants. But that concept has been discarded because of the need to assure proper dosage of a drug. Thus, substances from

Scientists no longer think that "edible vaccines" are practical. Today's pharma crops contain substances that can be used to manufacture medicines, like these red clover plants.

pharma plants need to be processed in order to manufacture a specific medicine in a prescribed amount.

Genetically modified rice, corn, tobacco, and some other plants can create large amounts of proteins found in humans. GE rice that contains human genes, for example, prompts the plant to make proteins found in human saliva, tears, and breast milk. The proteins can then be turned into products to treat stomach ailments.

Planting acres of GE pharma crops can cut production costs for medicinal drugs. So, along with Ventria, other companies are producing or planning to produce pharma crops, which could provide lower-cost drugs for consumers and profits for an industry that is expected to be worth more than $2 billion by 2011.[20]

Some of the potential products include pharmaceuticals to heal wounds and treat conditions such as anemia, cystic fibrosis, HIV, and other illnesses. Scientists have produced vaccines to protect against rabies, cholera, and other diseases. Anticoagulants, blood substitutes, and hormones are other possibilities from pharma crops. Many industrial compounds that modified plants produce are enzymes—proteins—that promote chemical reactions needed to manufacture such items as plastics, detergents, and paper. Chemicals used in research also come from pharma crops. Many scientists as well as food processors want the pharma crop industry to use nonfood plants like tobacco for chemical or pharmaceutical production. They also emphasize that strict regulation is needed for pharma crops and other experimental GE plants. Those regulations vary by country and by the agencies responsible for protecting food supplies.

6 **Regulating GE Crops**

As experts debate the benefits and possible risks of GMOs, who, you might ask, is checking on the safety of GE crops and foods? Since the United States produces more GE crops than any other country, does that mean the United States also has more and better safety regulations for GE foods than any other nation? That question also prompts debates. Opponents claim that U.S. regulation of GMOs is haphazard and negligent, while proponents argue that there are many safeguards in place.

In reality, there is a complex mix of U.S. laws and regulatory agencies as well as state statutes and local ordinances responsible for certain aspects of GE food and fiber development. In addition, if U.S.-grown GE crops are exported to other countries, they are subject to stringent regulations of the European Union and also those of some African and Asian countries. International regulatory bodies such as the World Trade Organization and the United Nations Food and Agriculture Organization also have a say about the trade and production of GE crops as does an international agreement known as the Cartagena Protocol on Biosafety.

U.S. Laws and the Regulators

Since the agbiotech industry began to commercialize GE crops in the United States, no new federal laws have been passed to regulate these products, although some regulations have become stricter, especially in regard to pharma crops. Instead of new statutes, the U.S. government established a formal policy called the "Coordinated Framework for Regulation of Biotechnology," which is a set of guidelines for regulating GE crops and food by using existing laws. These are the Plant Protection Act; the Federal Insecticide, Fungicide, and Rodenticide Act; the Toxic Substances Control Act; and Federal Food, Drug, and Cosmetic Act. In the view of the U.S. government, genetic modification of food crops is considered no different from traditional breeding of plants and animals.

The three main U.S. government agencies responsible for regulating the products of genetic engineering are the U.S. Department of Agriculture's Animal and Plant Health Inspection Service (USDA-APHIS), the U.S. Environmental Protection Agency (EPA), and the Department of Health and Human Services' Food and Drug Administration (FDA). In some cases, two or three agencies may review a product, depending on its traits and purpose. For example, the EPA regulates a Bt plant as a pesticide, but the USDA oversees any field trials of such a crop.

The FDA determines the safety of food, feed, food additives, veterinary drugs, human drugs, and medical devices. Years ago, the agency could have regulated GE products as additives, requiring that they be tested for allergens and toxic substances. However, the FDA regulates GE products under a provision known as GRAS (generally regarded as safe) of the federal Food, Drug, and Cosmetics Act. All companies planning to market a genetically modified crop are advised to consult with the FDA prior to release and to submit safety data related to the presence of natural toxins, potential allergens, nutritional value, stability of the inserted gene, and assessment of unintended effects. Nevertheless, some contend that GE products are not thoroughly tested and proven safe, as the U.S. government claims. David Schubert, a medical researcher at California's Salk Institute, says: "The picture that emerges from our study of U.S. regulation of GE foods is a rubber-stamp 'approval process' designed to increase public confidence in, but not ensure the safety of, genetically engineered foods." William Freese, a research analyst with the environmental organization Friends of the Earth, adds that "GM food regulation in the U.S. bears as little relation to good science as the typical used car ad to the true state of the automobile. Both are designed to sell a product."[1] An independent British study released earlier in the year came to similar conclusions regarding the safety of existing GE crops.

Opponents claim that U.S. regulation of GMOs is haphazard and negligent, while proponents argue that there are many safeguards in place.

A plant scientist, Alan McHughen, at University of California, Riverside disagrees. In an Agricultural and Bio-technology publication for the university, McHughen states:

> [GE] technology and its resulting products have always been highly regulated in the United States, and the scientific basis for the

regulatory oversight is under constant review by the scientific community as well as by the relevant federal and state government agencies. As a result, crops and foods derived from genetic engineering receive greater regulatory safety evaluation prior to commercial release than any other crops or foods in the history of agriculture. This regulatory framework ensures that the safety of genetically engineered crops is superior or at least comparable to the safety of conventionally produced crops, although regulatory costs for GE crops are much higher than for conventional ones.[2]

According to the government, its regulatory system is "transparent, predictable, open to public comment, and based on sound science. It is continuously reviewed and evaluated to ensure that it meets the challenges to this evolving technology."[3]

How U.S. States Regulate Biotech Crops

In the states, regulators enforce state laws that are similar to those that U.S. agencies administer. But the states have specific agricultural and economic concerns, and state officials say they, not federal agencies, are best able to promote and protect their economic interests in regard to planting GE crops and marketing them. "No issue involving biotech crops and foods has received more attention within state governments, the agricultural community, and from the media, than the technology's potential to hurt market access for conventional and organic crops," according to a report from the Pew Initiative on Food and Biotechnology.[4] The lengthy report issued in December 2004 also points out: "Whatever the local concern, it is more likely to be brought forcefully to bear at the state government level than at the federal level."[5]

That was evident in Alaska. In May 2005, Alaska's legislators unanimously passed the first law in the nation to compel the labeling of GE foods, a law that 90 percent of Americans want on a federal level.[6] The law requires that fish products be

This striped bass was not genetically engineered. Some states require that GE foods be labeled—to inform the consumer, protect the environment, and to guard a state's business interests.

labeled as genetically modified "by means that are not possible under natural conditions or processes."[7]

Even though no GE fish are yet on the market, Alaska lawmakers were prompted to pass the legislation because an aquaculture company, Aqua Bounty Technologies, has requested approval from the FDA to sell GE salmon. The company is breeding salmon that have been genetically modified to mature in about eighteen months, compared to the twenty-four to thirty months it takes salmon to reach maturity in the wild. One of the bill's sponsors was State Senator Gary Stevens (R-Kodiak), who declared: "This bill helps highlight Alaska seafood as distinct from genetically modified seafood." Labeling reinforces "the natural message," a message that he believes is a "highly important marketing tool."[8]

In addition, state officials may respond to environmental concerns, such as protecting wildlife from possible adverse effects of genetically modified organisms. In the case of engineered salmon on both the Alaskan and eastern coasts, some ecologists fear that if these GE fish were released or escaped into waterways, they may endanger native salmon. According to the Union of Concerned Scientists,

> Concerns about escape are well founded. Farmed salmon are traditionally grown in ocean netpens and these cages are not escape-proof. Storms and hungry animals can damage netpens, releasing large numbers of fish. Once out, the animals are virtually impossible to recapture.[9]

In other states, local jurisdictions in towns, cities, and counties have also proposed laws or passed resolutions to regulate GE foods. Anti-GE activists contend that local action is needed in order to counteract the lack of safety measures at the state and federal level. Many of the bills are attempts to prevent GE contamination of conventional farm crops or to protect human health and the environment. For example, in California, where there are no state regulations regarding GE crops, three counties—Marin, Mendocino, and Trinity—passed ordinances in 2004 banning the planting of GE seeds. Citizens voted down similar bans in other counties.

Opponents of local bans began efforts in 2004 to pass a preemptive law—that is, it would give the state of California authority to regulate seeds and in effect would block county bans on GE crops. Similar efforts are under way in other states, and at least fifteen have passed laws that prevent local governments or agencies from controlling crops: Arizona, Georgia, Florida, Idaho, Iowa, Indiana, Kansas, Michigan, North Dakota, Ohio, Oklahoma, Pennsylvania, South Dakota, Texas, and West Virginia.[10] Many state legislators argue that states should be responsible for determining what should or should not be grown; in their view, state regulations would be more consistent than local ones.

GE Regulations in Europe

The majority of Europeans have reservations about GE crops and foods, citing health, safety, and environmental concerns. The Eurobarometer survey for 2001 found that almost 86 percent want to know more about GE food products before eating them, and 95 percent want the right to choose whether to consume these products. Fifty-nine percent of Europeans believe that GMOs may have a negative effect on the environment. Yet that same percentage believe that science and technology can improve agriculture.[11]

Europeans are also wary of government officials who proclaim their food is safe, primarily because of crises that have developed, although the problems have been unrelated to GMOs. For example, bovine spongiform encephalopathy, or "mad cow disease," developed during the 1980s; it began in Britain and spread to the rest of Europe, killing animals and people who ate infected meat.

Other highly publicized agricultural catastrophes included meat in Belgium that was contaminated with dioxin and animals across Europe with foot-and-mouth disease. After these events, many people feared their government could not protect the safety of their country's food supply.[12]

Since the early 1990s, the European Union has developed regulations for GMOs. The EU has the authority to legislate on a variety of issues affecting its members, and it banned the import of new GE products between 1998 and 2004, although field trials of GE crops and GMOs have taken place in some European countries.

In the meantime, the United States, Canada, and Argentina charged that the European Union was blocking free trade by restricting GMOs. The United States asked the World Trade Organization to rule on its claim. The WTO was created in 1994 as a result of the international General Agreement on Tariffs and Trade (GATT). The WTO has the authority to force national governments to modify laws and environmental standards to promote free trade.

Partly to avoid a trade conflict with the United States, the EU executive commission, backed by Britain, in effect lifted the ban in 2004, allowing several varieties of insect- and herbicide-resistant GE corn to be planted or imported for animal and human consumption. The commission also attempted to gain approval to plant more GE crops in Europe. But five EU nations—Austria, Luxembourg, Germany, France, and Greece—have continued to impose a blanket ban on GE products in spite of pressure from the EU commission, the WTO, and the United States. In addition, a report in *The New York Times* in June 2006 points out that both consumers and growers in these five EU countries continue to resist and to ban GE crops within their borders.[13]

EU rules put into effect in 2004 require that human food and animal feeds that have GE ingredients bear a GE label

Protesters in Vienna, Austria, demonstrate against GE food outside an agriculture conference. The majority of Europeans polled have concerns about the safety of genetically engineered foods.

clearly stating the name of GMOs used at each stage of production. The purpose of the label is to provide consumers with information that allows them to identify GE products and make a choice about whether to buy them.

GE Regulations in Other Nations

If you were to look for GMO regulations around the globe, you would likely find dozens of rule variations. Besides European labeling regulations, such countries as New Zealand, China, Japan, and Saudi Arabia also require labels on GE crops, as do the South American countries Brazil, Chile, and Ecuador.

In Australia, the national government approved the planting of GE canola, but the states of New South Wales, South Australia, Tasmania, Victoria, Western Australia, and the Australian Capital Territory have bans that prevent the planting of GE canola. Queensland is the only state that does not have a ban, but rapeseed is not grown there.

In some parts of the world, areas or regions are declared GE-free. Most of these are in Europe and include communities in Belgium, Germany, and Italy, according to the Center for Food Safety, which has an ongoing effort to chart regulations for GE crops and foods.[14]

Some countries have no regulations at all in regard to GMOs. Some are in the process of passing laws and setting up regulations to assure safe use, handling, and transport of GMOs, a requirement of an international set of rules known as the Cartagena Protocol on Biosafety.

More than 130 countries have adopted the Cartagena Protocol, named for Cartagena, Colombia, where it was initiated in 1999. Adopted in 2000, it became effective in 2003.

The purpose of the protocol is to help ensure the safe movement of GMOs across national borders and to conserve and sustain biological diversity—protect the variety of living things in a given area. Biodiversity may be at risk from GMOs, or living modified organisms (LMOs), the term used in the protocol. This legally binding agreement requires that countries receive advance notification of GMO imports and related scientific risk assessments before genetically modified products are introduced into an environment.

No matter what the regulations or where they are in effect, however, there is political pressure on regulatory and judicial systems to allow GE products or to ban them. In fact, some observers believe that politics plays a major role in how the legal and scientific arguments regarding status of GMOs are framed.

The Politics of GMOs

Abolish Biotech Now

GMOs Here to Stay

These slogans on two competing signs represent opposite positions in the GE debate and indicate how lines are drawn. Played out in the political arena, the GMO controversy has sometimes become a bumper-sticker battle, and even the words used can mean one thing for the proponents' side and another for the opponents'.

Consider the word "purity" as it applies to GMOs. Guy Cook, a linguist and author of *Genetically Modified Language*, puts it this way: "For the pro-GM lobby, genetic modification is a way of achieving purity, uncontaminated by weeds or pests; for the anti-GE lobby it is the genetically *un*modified which is pure, and the introduction of new genetic material which is the impurity."[1]

Throughout his book, Cook analyzes the many ways that people talk and write about the same thing, leading to misunderstandings in regard to GMOs. He shows how the GE debate has become "a war of words, to be won as much by persuasion as by action in the laboratory, field or supermarket."[2]

Catchy slogans about GMOs do indeed get more attention from the public than what experts say or write. The "Frankenfood" term is one that shows up often, and both sides in the debate about GMOs use it. The reference sometimes makes headlines, such as "Can Frankenstein Foods Harm Your Baby?" or in quotes like British Prime Minister Tony Blair's words: "I eat Frankenstein food and it's safe."[3]

One of the reasons slogans and sound-bite phrases dominate in the media is that few of us have the background to know whether the pronouncements of various scientists, economists, sociologists, ethicists, or others presenting academic studies and GMO data are accurate. Besides that, the experts may disagree with each other, leaving most people wondering who is right and what to believe.

Corporate Politics

Agbiotech corporations employ numerous tactics to get their pro-GE messages across to governments, regulators, and populations worldwide. Corporations lobby government officials and launch public relations and advertising campaigns, touting the benefits of some modified crops.

One campaign got under way in 2000 when a Swiss research team announced they had genetically modified rice to produce beta-carotene, an essential nutrient with a yellow pigment that converts to vitamin A in the body. (Regular white rice has no beta-carotene, and brown rice contains only a small amount.) Quickly dubbed "golden rice," developers at the biotech company Syngenta said the rice would help 125,000 to 150,000 children worldwide who have a vitamin A deficiency that leads to irreversible blindness, and perhaps prevent the deaths of children who have weakened immune systems due to the lack of beta-carotene.

In the debate over GE foods, even the words used—such as "purity"—can mean one thing for the proponents' side and another thing for the opponents'.

When news broke about the development of golden rice, "the politics of the experiment were even more significant than the science," wrote Peter Pringle in *Food, Inc.* "The biotech industry seized the moment, launching a TV advertising blitz that trumpeted the possibilities to end world hunger and disease."[4] For weeks, media stories praised the discovery and predicted that the modified rice and other GE crops would solve global malnutrition problems.

Yet achieving the promise of golden rice is a long way off, for several reasons:

1. Humanitarian efforts for developing countries are not the first priority for agbiotech companies; rather, efforts are geared toward GE crops for industrialized nations where research and development can pay off with profits.

2. There are other food sources of vitamin A (such as carrots and other vegetables) and supplements that would be less expensive to provide than golden rice, but poor people do not have the means to obtain these products.

3. People need to have a diverse diet, which includes fat, in order to absorb beta-carotene, and tests are still being conducted to determine whether the beta-carotene in the grains alone can be absorbed and used by the human body.

Nevertheless, additional experiments with GE rice have increased the beta-carotene content, and in 2005, development companies offered the rice free to Asian research centers for field trials. Perhaps the experimental rice will regain its golden glow and once more be the poster child for pro-GE campaigns. Like many other aspects of the GE debate, that remains to be seen.

Lobbying Efforts

In the meantime, agbiotech firms press their agendas through government agencies in the United States and elsewhere, and agencies cooperate because they see economic benefits in selling GE crops and foods. Various aid organizations (such as the United States Agency for International Development and the United Nations World Food Programme) and some farmers' groups also promote the economic advantages of planting GE crops.

One of the major lobbying groups for biotech companies is the Biotechnology Industry Organization (BIO) founded in 1993. With headquarters in Washington, D.C., "BIO represents more than 1,100 biotechnology companies, academic institutions, state biotechnology centers and related organizations across the United States and 31 other nations," according to its president, Jim Greenwood. One mission of BIO is to shape political and public views about GMOs not only by lobbying but also by testifying before Congress. For example, Greenwood appeared before Congress in mid-2005 at a Senate Committee on Agriculture, Nutrition, and Forestry that was reviewing future agriculture and food biotechnology developments. Greenwood testified along with USDA, EPA, and FDA officials, the chairman of the American Soybean Association, and others about the importance of biotechnology. He noted in part:

> The rapid adoption of this technology by U.S. farmers is a testament to the solutions it provides to problems on the farm. Biotechnology enables farmers to reduce input costs and improve

yields. And by freeing farmers from the chore of constantly spraying and tilling their fields to remove weeds, biotech improved crops not only reduce the use of chemical inputs, reduce soil erosion, and reduce the use of fossil fuels; they increase the amount of time farmers have to spend with their families.[5]

Comparable organizations with similar purposes have been established in Africa (AfricaBio), Australia (AusBiotech), Europe (EuropaBio), India (All India Biotech Association), New Zealand (New Zealand Biotechnology Association), Canada (BIOTECanada), and others. Usually, the general public hears or reads little about these organizations, except when international conferences or conventions are held, such as the 2005 BIO conference in Philadelphia that drew thousands of anti-GE protesters. Another major player in the political arena is the nonprofit foundation known as AgBioWorld, founded in 2000 in the United States by a Tuskegee (Alabama) University professor, Channapatna Prakash, and Gregory Conko of the Competitive Enterprise Institute, a nonprofit organization that advocates for free enterprise and limited government. The two established an Internet site to organize scientists and get them to sign the "Declaration of Scientists in Support of Biotechnology," which has been widely publicized. The site also says that its free electronic newsletter provides "research updates and commentary for anyone interested in the latest on advances in plant science, agricultural research and sustainable food production."[6]

Articles by Prakash and studies in support of GE crops and foods have also been posted on the site. His "efforts have made him an oft-quoted celebrity of the biotech wars and won him invitations to carry the industry's banner at biotech forums around the world," according to author Bill Lambrecht.[7]

Many other supporters of biotechnology and GE products are quoted in the media, and some are likely to dismiss anti-GE groups as zealots or Frankenfood freaks. Supporters say that

Children in Angola wait at a food distribution center. People disagree about whether GE food is a solution to the world's hunger problems.

genetically modified farming is more efficient than traditional farming because fewer crops are lost to weeds and pests. This, they say, will expand export markets and feed more people worldwide.

Anti-GE Political Action

Political messages from GMO opponents often emphasize that agbiotech companies are only concerned about profits and not the possible negative effects on people and the environment. Opponents charge that cultural and social issues are not taken into account when GE crops are promoted. In its controversial report *Selling Suicide*, Christian Aid stated that too much significance is placed on GE crops in terms of their ability to end hunger in the developing world. In addition, the report argues that

- Too much control over the world's agriculture and food system ends up in the hands of a small number of purely economic interests.

- Alternatives to GE crops are receiving too few resources in terms of agricultural research and support to farmers.

- Too much pressure is being applied and too little time and assistance is being given to developing countries to help them properly debate and decide for themselves whether to use GE crops.[8]

Groups also try to alert the public to the increasing power of multinational corporations and their control of agriculture and food production, emphasizing the need to support local farmers who have little political influence. Dozens of other international organizations have ongoing anti-GMO campaigns trying to influence government policies in many countries. Some of the organization names are familiar such as Greenpeace, Friends of the Earth International, and the Sierra Club. Others are lesser known opponents who have organized and created attention-getting campaigns. Some examples:

- In 2003, New Zealand chefs, food writers, restaurant owners, and wine makers launched the PureFoodNZ campaign to urge that the country remain GE free.

- In 2004, activists for Friends of the Earth's Real Food campaign in Great Britain dressed up as scarecrows (traditional crop protectors) or set up scarecrow icons to alert the public about possible GE contamination and to call for strict regulation of GE crops.

- In 2005, the Trade Association released an Internet science-fiction film called *Store Wars: the Organic Rebellion*. A lighthearted spoof of *Star Wars*, it features live-action puppets created from organic vegetables, fruits, and pastries with names like Cuke Skywalker, Princess Lettuce, Chewbroccoli, and other organic rebels who battle with Darth Tader (a potato), the evil lord of the Dark Side of the Farm, where, as the story goes, pesticide use and GE crops must be overcome.[9]

The Organic Connection

As the *Store Wars* film suggests, organic food growers, producers, and consumers are among the anti-GE forces trying to influence government policies on agriculture. For years, the term "organic" has referred to plants and animals free of synthetic chemicals, but because organic applies to anything made up of carbon, the label could be placed on virtually any food. There was no specific definition for the term, and no standards were set until 2000, when the USDA issued regulations for organic products. Today, no foods can be labeled organic if they are produced using specific genetic engineering tools such as recombinant DNA—but they do permit "cell culture" and other technologies. They must also be free of irradiation and antibiotics.

According to the Organic Consumers Association (OCA), 50 million Americans now buy certified organic foods, even though they can cost up to twice as much as conventional foods. The OCA's director declares:

> Organic consumers believe that higher grocery bills . . . are well worth it, since [organic] producers are raising crops and animals the traditional way—without dangerous pesticides, chemical fertilizers, animal drugs, hormones, tainted animal feed, or genetically engineered seeds.[10]

Many organic food producers across the United States—usually on small or medium-sized farms—are attempting to fill the increasing demand for organic products. But in some

Organic farmers inspect a field of red chard in California. Many people prefer organic food because it is produced without irradiation, pesticides, or genetic engineering.

areas, they must also spend time, effort, and money to protect their crops because pollen from GE crops grown on large industrialized farms nearby could contaminate their produce.

At times, organic farmers fight political battles to get local or state laws passed to establish GE-free farming areas. Frequently, organic food consumers join farmers in these political fights not only in the United States but also in other nations. Why? Partly because the demand for organic foods is growing worldwide.

According to a market research report "Current Organic Agriculture Market Worldwide: A Year in View (2005)":

> One of the key factors behind this growth is the increasing consumer awareness of health and environmental issues along with an increasing resistance towards genetically modified food products and GE farming. . . . More than 26 million hectares [more than 64 million acres] of lands worldwide are certified "organic" and are generating more than US $25 billion in revenue. . . . More than 560,000 farms in more than 108 countries are currently certified.[11]

In spite of the expansion of organic farming, the trend for using GE products in processed foods will likely continue if advocates have their way. However, critics are likely to go on with their efforts to sway opinion in the opposite direction. In short, the debate has not ended. It includes arguments over food labels and choices for consumers, who in the end may play a significant role in what kinds of foods are produced.

Consumer Views and Choices

Consumers around the world want information about the food they buy and eat, which raises the question: Should the packaged food label indicate that the product includes GE ingredients? The issue is under discussion—sometimes heated discussion—in many countries.

A 2003 National Consumer Council (NCC) survey in Great Britain found that the public was uneasy about GMOs and commercialization of them. In the survey, 60 percent of consumers said they feared that genetic engineering interfered with nature and that they did not believe their government was truthful about the safety of GE foods. Consumers also said they had the right to know whether their food is produced with GE crops or animals fed with GE feed. In addition, a majority of consumers surveyed viewed "GM companies, food manufacturers and farmers as the potential beneficiaries of GM technology" while only 5 percent thought consumers would benefit.[1]

Global Requirements for GE Labels

At the present time, more than forty countries require labeling of GE products. These include the twenty-five countries of the European Union, the Latin American countries of Brazil, Chile, and Colombia, plus Australia, South Africa, Saudi Arabia, and some Asian countries, including Japan, China, and South Korea.[2]

In May 2005, representatives of fifty-five countries met in Malaysia to discuss global labeling standards for genetically engineered foods. The delegates were members of Codex Alimentarius Commission, which was created in 1963 by the United Nations Food and Agriculture Organization and the World Health Organization. Called Codex for short, the commission was established to set standards and guidelines for global food safety, fair food trade practices, and worldwide consumer protection.

Members of Consumers International (CI) were at the Codex meeting to lobby for GE labels. CI contends that Codex guidelines are needed to protect countries that label GE food and are threatened with disputes about unfair trade practices. Developing countries also need guidance if they want to introduce laws on GE labels.

At the 2005 meeting, thirty countries supported standards for GE labels, but the United States, Australia, Argentina, and four other nations pressed to end the discussions, according to news reports. Delegates from eighteen countries did not comment on the issue, and the meeting adjourned without any decision. In effect, the United States, which is the top supplier of GE foods worldwide, and six other countries were able to stop any progress on GE labels.[3]

Labeling a Pizza

To explain how labeling works in European countries, the organization Agricultural Biotechnology in Europe (ABE), a communications organization for the agricultural biotechnology industry, created a consumer booklet that shows who along the food supply chain is required to label products. The booklet illustrates the process with ingredients used to make a popular food: pizza. It begins with tomato purée on the pizza, for which there are no label requirements because no GE tomato seeds are allowed to be sold in Europe. If, however, GE tomatoes were used, the tomato processor would be required by law to label the purée as genetically engineered, and the merchant would have to label the pizza saying it contains GE ingredients.[4]

What about meat and cheese on a pizza? Animal products—meat, milk, and eggs—do not have to be labeled along the food supply chain, with one exception: producers of animal feed. The diet of farm animals in Europe usually includes GE soybeans and corn, so feed producers must indicate the GE content on a label.

Vegetable oil is a pizza ingredient that must be labeled along almost every step of the food supply chain, if the oil is derived from GE soybeans, canola, corn, or cottonseed. In other words, seed suppliers, farmers who harvest GE grain, seed crushers, pizza manufacturers, and retailers are legally required to indicate on a label that the vegetable oil comes from a GE source.

U.S. Consumer Views

In the United States, the Pew Initiative on Food and Biotechnology conducted a survey of consumers in 2004, its third to record views on genetic engineering in agriculture. The first survey in 2001 tracked consumer awareness of GM crops,

Surveys have found that the vast majority of Americans believe that GE food should be labeled. However, trade groups argue that such labeling would provide little information to consumers.

and the 2003 survey also examined issues such as regulation of GE foods. The third survey included focus groups—bringing together people in Philadelphia, Pennsylvania, and Des Moines, Iowa, to discuss their views about GMOs. In summary, the Pew Initiative noted:

> Americans remain relatively uninformed about genetically modified foods and the application of genetic engineering technology to agriculture. . . . What knowledge consumers do have appears to be driven mostly by the degree to which the media concentrates on the issue.

In spite of little knowledge about GE foods—or perhaps because of it—labeling was a top priority of U.S. consumers surveyed. Ninety-two percent supported labeling GE food, and 91 percent said GE ingredients in processed foods should be labeled.[5]

Even so, a representative of the Grocery Manufacturers of America contends that labeling GE foods provides little information of value to consumers. The food industry fears that a GE label would be like a red flag—a warning that the product is unsafe—and would frighten away some consumers. What is more important, manufacturers say, is that genetically produced food is as safe and as healthy as the conventionally grown varieties, and the product itself ought to be assessed for safety rather than the growing process. If labels say that GE ingredients are used, for example, the information should include the fact that the World Health Organization, the United Nations' Food and Agriculture Organization, and various national governments have found genetically engineered products to be as safe as conventional foods.

A countering argument from the Consumers Choice Council is that if genetic modification of food is beneficial, then producers should be willing to label food as such. The council says consumers have the right to know, and it supports mandatory federal labeling for all GE foods.[6]

Being a GE Sleuth

When you buy food, do you look at the label on a package, can, or bottle? If so, you know that the serving size is at the top of a label. Below it, the calories and other items are listed per serving. At the bottom of most labels is a list of Daily Values for those who eat 2,000 or 2,500 calories daily. This is a guide to help you get 100 percent of the vitamins and minerals you need each day (from a variety of foods) and to help you limit the amount of fat, sugar, and sodium (salt) you consume. In some supermarkets, nutrients and calories are listed on produce shelves for a great variety of fresh fruits and vegetables. The labels on packaged meats, poultry, and fish indicate calories, fat, and protein amounts. Knowing the nutrient content of your food helps you make healthy food choices.

But what about ingredients that are genetically engineered? You will not find them listed as such on labels. However, you may find clues. If you want to be a GE sleuth, you can check out some foods on cupboard shelves or in the refrigerator in your own home.

More than forty countries require labeling of GE products. In the United States, where labeling is not required, 92 percent of those surveyed support it.

For example, you can get information about fresh produce on one of the tiny stickers attached to an apple, orange, banana, kiwi, melon, tomato, squash, papaya, and various other fruits and vegetables. The sticker includes a PLU code, which stands for "price look-up." The code was designed as a way to help clerks check on prices for specific types of fresh produce and also to indicate whether they are organic, conventional, or genetically modified.

For instance, an apple could have the code 4131, a lemon 4053, and a head of lettuce 4061. A four-digit number indicates the type of produce and that it is conventionally grown. If the same produce is organically grown, there is a five-digit number beginning with the numeral 9 (94131, 94053, or 94061, for

The stickers on fresh produce can tell shoppers whether it is genetically engineered or not, but the system is not mandatory.

example.) A five-digit number beginning with the numeral 8 is supposed to appear on produce that has been genetically modified.[7]

In the mid-1990s, when this numbering system was developed, the Produce Marketing Association believed that GE fruits and vegetables would be in great demand in the near future. But that has not happened. In fact, very few fruits and vegetables are genetically modified for commercial purposes.

Papayas are one exception. Papayas have been modified to resist a virus that destroys the fruit, but they are not labeled as GE. Rather, they may be considered the same as the conventional variety and carry the four-digit number—or none at all. Why? Because the PLU system is strictly voluntary and grocers may opt not to use it.

In your home, you may find foods that you know are not genetically modified because they are certified organic products or purchased from stores like Whole Foods and Trader Joe's. Since 2003, most of Trader Joe's foods are not derived from GE products; its company-brand foods especially are GE free and sold in its two hundred stores in nineteen states. The company says it has "identified any product containing ingredients that could potentially be derived from genetically engineered crops and worked with our suppliers" to provide alternatives.[8]

As for the foods in your home, you can check the ingredients in processed foods, and determine whether they contain corn-, soy-, rapeseed (canola)- or cottonseed-based products. If so, it is likely that they are genetically modified. To make sure, you might have to get in touch with the manufacturer of the product. (Usually, their toll-free numbers are listed on a can or jar label or package.) Also, some organizations like Greenpeace's True Food Network offer lists of non-GE and genetically modified processed foods.[9]

Whether or not you and other consumers are concerned about GE foods and labels or about any GMOs, the choices we all make in what we eat may have an effect on how food is produced in the future. Currently, though, there is no evidence that genetic modification of foods will stop. Nor is there any sign that opponents will be muffled. That means unless there are frank, objective, public discussions about food production in the future, most of us will have to determine for ourselves the benefits and risks of GE foods.

Chapter Notes

Chapter 1   What's in a Name?

1. Jeffrey Kaye, "Pigs and Politics," *Online NewsHour*, June 3, 2004, <http://www.pbs.org/newshour/bb/science/jan-june04/pigs_6-3.html> (June 8, 2006).

2. William K. Hallman, W. Carl Hebden, Cara L. Cuite, Helen L. Aquino, and John T. Lang, *Americans and GM Food: Knowledge, Opinion and Interest in 2004* (New Brunswick, N.J.: Food Policy Institute, Cook College/Rutgers, The State University of New Jersey, November 2004), p. 1.

3. Union of Concerned Scientists, "What Is Biotechnology?" July 18, 2003, <http://www.ucsusa.org/food_and_environment/biotechnology/page.cfm?pageID=340> (June 8, 2006).

4. Larry Thompson, "Are Bioengineered Foods Safe?" *FDA Consumer*, January-February 2000, <http://www.fda.gov/fdac/features/2000/100_bio.html> (June 8, 2006).

5. Rutgers University Food Policy Institute, "Genetically Modified Food—Frequently Asked Questions," 2002, <http://www.biotech.foodpolicyinstitute.org/overview.html> (June 8, 2006).

6. Guelph Transgenic Pig Research Program, n.d., <http://www.uoguelph.ca/enviropig/> (June 8, 2006).

7. Peter Pringle, *Food, Inc.: Mendel to Monsanto—The Promises and Perils of the Biotech Harvest* (New York: Simon & Schuster, 2003), p. 122.

8. Hallman, Hebden, Cuite, Aquino, and Lang.

9. Ibid.; see also Rutgers University Food Policy Institute.

Chapter 2   The First Modified Foods

1. "Puzzle of Corn's Origins Coming Together," EurekAlert!, Duke University, press release, April 8, 2004, <http://www.eurekalert.org/pub_releases/2004-04/du-poc033004.php> (June 8, 2006).

2. Dawn A. Tamarkin, "Introduction to Genetics," *Principles of Biology I*, Springfield (Massachusetts) Technical Community

College, STCC Foundation Press, November 14, 2003, <http://distance.stcc.edu/BIOL102/Lectures/lesson2/genetics1.htm> (June 8, 2006).

3. "Hybrid Crops," *Wessels Living History Farm, Farming in the 1930s,* n.d., <http://www.livinghistoryfarm.org/farminginthe30s/crops_02.html> (June 8, 2006).

4. Peter Pringle, *Food, Inc.: Mendel to Monsanto—The Promises and Perils of the Biotech Harvest* (New York: Simon & Schuster, 2003), p. 47.

Chapter 3 Production of GE Food

1. USDA Economic Research Service, "Adoption of Genetically Engineered Crops in the United States," July 13, 2005, <http://www.ers.usda.gov/Data/BiotechCrops/adoption.htm> (June 8, 2006).

2. The International Service for the Acquisition of Agri-biotech Applications, "Global Status of Commercialized Biotech/GM Crops: 2004," <http://www.isaaa.org/kc/bin/ESummary/index.htm> (May 18, 2006).

3. USDA Economic Research Service.

4. The International Service for the Acquisition of Agri-biotech Applications, "Worldwide Biotech Crops Experience Near Record Growth," press release, January 12, 2005; see also The International Service for the Acquisition of Agri-biotech Applications.

5. Pew Initiative on Food and Biotechnology, "Genetically Modified Crops in the United States," August 2004, <http://pewagbiotech.org/resources/factsheets/display.php3?FactsheetID=2> (June 8, 2006).

6. Henry I. Miller and Gregory Conko, "Biotech Woes and the Culprits," *Washington Times,* June 24, 2003, <http://washingtontimes.com/commentary/20030623-084137-3315r.htmc> (June 8, 2006).

7. Monsanto, "Products and Solutions: Setting the Standard in the Field," n.d., <http://www.monsanto.com/monsanto/layout/products/default.asp> (June 8, 2006).

8. Cheryl Alberts, "Roundup Ready Soybeans Have Yield Trade-off," *Research Nebraska*, September 2000, <http://ard.unl.edu/rn/0900/bean.html> (June 29, 2006).

9. "Peppers," Tough Love Chile Company, 2005, <http://www.tough-love.com/seed_descriptions.html#PRAIRIE%20FIRE> (June 29, 2006).

10. Bill Lambrecht, *Dinner at the New Gene Café* (New York: Thomas Dunne Books/St. Martin's Press, 2001), p. 101.

11. David Canton, "Seed Patents Hit Farmers," *London Free Press*, February 19, 2005, <http://www.canoe.ca/NewsStand/Columnists/London/Business_Law/David_Canton/2005/02/19/935570.html> (August 1, 2005); see also *Monsanto* vs. *U.S. Farmers*, Report by the Center for Food Safety, 2005, Executive Summary, p. 4, <http://www.centerforfoodsafety.org/Monsantovsusfarmersreport.cfm> (June 8, 2006).

12. *Monsanto* vs. *U.S. Farmers.*

13. Drew L. Kershen, "Monsanto vs. U.S. Farmers: Commentary on the Center for Food Safety Report," April 2005, <http://www.isb.vt.edu/articles/apr0504.htm> (May 19, 2006).

14. Cecil H. Yancy, Jr., "Saved Seed Proved to Be Expensive," *Southeast Farm Press*, June 18, 2003, <http://southeastfarmpress.com/mag/farming_saved_seed_proved/> (June 8, 2006).

15. Ibid.

16. Percy Schmeiser, "Percy Schmeiser vs. Monsanto," n.d., <http://www.percyschmeiser.com/> (June 8, 2006).

17. Cornell Cooperative Extension, "Percy Schmeiser: Canola Crook or Corporate Martyr?" Genetically Engineered Organisms Public Issues Education (GEO-PIE) Project, August 16, 2004, <http://www.geo-pie.cornell.edu/issues/schmeiser.html> (June 8, 2006).

18. "Monsanto Canada Inc. and Monsanto Company Plaintiffs and Percy Schmeiser and Schmeiser Enterprises Ltd. Defendants," March 29, 2001, p. 61, <http://www.geo-pie.cornell.edu/issues/schmeister_appeal.pdf> (June 8, 2006).

19. Percy Schmeiser, "Percy Schmeiser Claims Moral and Personal

Victory in Supreme Court Decision," May 22, 2004, <http://www.percyschmeiser.com/decisioncomments.htm> (June 8, 2006).

Chapter 4   Opposing and Protesting GE Products

1. Jeremy Smith, Reuters, "EU Authorises GMO Maize Type by Legal Rubberstamp," August 8, 2005, <http://www.planetark.com/dailynewsstory.cfm/newsid/31971/story.htm> (June 8, 2006).

2. Paula Park, "Protests Hit BIO Meeting—Protestors and Industry Wage Rhetorical Battles over the Pros and Cons of GM Crops," *The Scientist*, June 9, 2004, <http://www.the-scientist.com/news/20040609/02> (August 2005).

3. Christian Aid, "Selling Suicide—Farming, False Promises and Genetic Engineering In Developing Countries," May 1999, <http://www.christian-aid.org.uk/indepth/9905suic/suicide2.htm#biotechnology> (May 25, 2006).

4. Ibid.

5. ETC Group, "Canadian Government to Unleash Terminator Bombshell at UN Meeting: All-out Push for Commercialisation of Sterile Seed Technology," news release, February 7, 2005, <http://www.etcgroup.org/documents/NR_SBSTTA10.Terminator.pdf> (June 8, 2006).

6. Union of Concerned Scientists, "Risks of Genetic Engineering," October 30, 2002, <http://www.ucsusa.org/food_and_environment/biotechnology/page.cfm?pageID=346> (May 25, 2006).

7. Greenpeace, "First On-Line Worldwide Register of GM Contamination Incidents Launched Today," news release, June 1, 2005.

8. Pew Initiative on Food and Biotechnology, "Journal and Mexican Government Disagree over Corn Contamination," April 30, 2002, <http://pewagbiotech.org/buzz/display.php3?StoryID=55> (May 20, 2006).

9. Ibid.

10. Ibid.

11. Ibid.

12. Holly Wagner, "Genetically Modified Maize Not Found in Southern Mexico," *Ohio State Research News*, press release, August 9, 2005. See also United Press International, "No U.S. GM Corn Is Found in Oaxaca," *Washington Times*, August 8, 2005, <http://washington times.com/upi/20050808-053954-1187r.htm> (June 8, 2006).

13. S. Ortiz-García, E. Ezcurra, B. Schoel, F. Acevedo, J. Soberó and A. A. Snow, "Absence of Detectable Transgenes in Local Landraces of Maize in Oaxaca, Mexico (2003–2004), *Proceedings of the National Academy of Sciences*, August 10, 2005, p. 5, <http://www. pnas.org/cgi/reprint/0503356102v1?maxtoshow=&HITS=10&hits =10&RESULTFORMAT=&fulltext=mexico+and+maize&searchid =1124544155008_1174&stored_search=&FIRSTINDEX=0&jour nalcode=pnas> (May 20, 2006).

14. Pew Initiative on Food and Biotechnology, *Three Years Later: Genetically Engineered Corn and the Monarch Butterfly Controversy*, 2002, p. 8.

15. Mark K. Sears, Richard L. Hellmich, Diane E. Stanley-Horn, Karen S. Oberhauser, John M. Pleasants, Heather R. Mattila, Blair D. Siegfried, and Galen P. Dively, "Impact of Bt Corn Pollen On Monarch Butterfly Populations: A Risk Assessment," Proceedings of the National Academy of Sciences of the United States of America, published online before print September 14, 2001 (published in PNAS October 9, 2001, pp. 11937–11942), <http://www.pnas.org/cgi/content/full/98/21/11937?maxtoshow= &HITS=10&hits=10&RESULTFORMAT=&fulltext=Bt+ monarch+butterflies&searchid=1123260495544_25665&stored_ search=&FIRSTINDEX=0&journalcode=pnas> (June 8, 2006).

16. David A. Bohan, Caroline W. H. Boffey, David R. Brooks, Suzanne J. Clark, Alan M. Dewar, Les G. Firbank, Alison J. Haughton, Cathy Hawes, Matthew S. Heard, Mike J. May, Juliet L. Osborne, Joe N. Perry, Peter Rothery, David B. Roy, Rod J. Scott, Geoff R. Squire, Ian P. Woiwod, and Gillian T. Champion, "Effects on Weed and Invertebrate Abundance and Diversity of Herbicide Management in Genetically Modified Herbicide-Tolerant Winter-Sown Oilseed Rape," *Proceedings of the Royal Society B*, March 7, 2005, pp. 463–474, <http://www.mindfully.

org/GE/2005/Bohan-Weed-Invertebrate7mar05.htm> (May 24, 2006).

17. Steve Connor, Michael McCarthy, and Colin Brown, "The End for GM Crops," *Independent*, March 22, 2005, <http://www. globalpolicy.org/socecon/trade/gmos/2005/0322endforgm.htm> (June 8, 2006).

18. Cornell Cooperative Extension's Genetically Engineered Organisms Public Issues Education (GEO-PIE) Project, "Genetically Engineered Foods: StarLink Corn in Taco Shells," May 3, 2003, <http://www.geo-pie.cornell.edu/educators/downloads/fs3_ starlink.pdf> (June 8, 2006) .

19. J. Lynne Brown, "Starlink," Biotechnology: Food and Agriculture, Penn State College of Agricultural Science, n.d., <http://biotech. cas.psu.edu/articles/starlink.htm> (May 20, 2006).

20. Jessica Azulay, "Anheuser-Busch Joins Fight Against Controversial 'Pharma Crops,'" *The New Standard*, April 14, 2005, <http:// newstandardnews.net/content/?action=show_item&itemid=1683> (June 8, 2006).

21. Jim Wasserman, "Biotech Rice Company Moves Again," *Sacramento Bee*, April 30, 2005, <http://www.ncsu.edu/news/dailyclips/0505/ 050205.htm#DJ7> (June 8, 2006).

Chapter 5   Reaping the Benefits of GMOs

1. World Health Organization, "Modern Food Biotechnology, Human Health and Development," June 23, 2005, p. v., <http:// www.who.int/foodsafety/publications/biotech/biotech_en.pdf> (June 8, 2006).

2. AgBioWorld, "Scientists In Support Of Agricultural Biotechnology," 2005, <http://www.agbioworld.org/declaration/petition/petition. php> (June 8, 2006).

3. Council for Biotechnology Information, "Good Ideas Are Growing—Plant Biotechnology," November 2002, p. 6, <http:// whybiotech.com/html/pdf/GoodIdeas-96dpi.pdf> (May 25, 2006).

4. Sujatha Sankula and Edward Blumenthal, "Impacts on US Agriculture of Biotechnology-Derived Crops Planted in 2003–

An Update of Eleven Case Studies," National Center for Food and Agriculture Policy, October 2004, p. 92, <http://www.ncfap.org/whatwedo/pdf/2004finalreport.pdf> (June 8, 2006).

5. American Soybean Association, National Corn Growers Association, National Cotton Council Of America, "One-Billionth Biotech Acre: Farmer Leaders Recognize Planting of One-Billionth Biotech Acre," news release, May 9, 2005, <http://www.soygrowers.com/biotech/r050905.htm> (May 17, 2006).

6. Council for Biotechnology Information, "Farmers From Around the World Praise Biotech Crops," 2004, <http://www.whybiotech.com/index.asp?id=4714> (June 8, 2006).

7. Anthony Shelton, "Preserving the Effectiveness of Bt Plants," ISB News Report, September 2005, <http://www.isb.vt.edu/news/2005/artspdf/sep0501.pdf> (May 22, 2006).

8. Susan Milius, "Bt Cotton: Yields Up in India; Pests Low in Arizona," *Science News Online*, February 8, 2003, <http://www.sciencenews.org/articles/20030208/fob5.asp> (May 22, 2006).

9. Richard Fawcett and Dan Towrey, "Conservation Tillage and Plant Biotechnology: How New Technologies Can Improve the Environment by Reducing the Need to Plow," A Biotech Paper, Purdue University Conservation Technology Information Center, 2002, <http://www.ctic.purdue.edu/CTIC/BiotechPaper.pdf> (May 22, 2006). (May 22, 2006).

10. Paul Driessen and Cyril Boynes, Jr., "Facts vs. Fears on Biotechnology: Misplaced Opposition to GM Crops Violates Poor People's Basic Human Rights," *CanadaFreePress.com,* March 9, 2005, <http://www.canadafreepress.com/2005/driessen030905.htm> (June 8, 2006).

11. Paul Driessen and Cyril Boynes, Jr., "Africans Have a Dream— Biotechnology Could Bring Health and Wealth to Africa," *Eco Imperialism,* February 17, 2005, <http://www.eco-imperialism.com/?a=article&id=115> (May 25, 2006).

12. Ibid.

13. Ibid.

14. Ibid.

15. Abraham McLaughlin and Christian Allen Purefoy, "Hunger Is Spreading in Africa," *Christian Science Monitor,* August 1, 2005, <http://www.csmonitor.com/2005/0801/p01s02-woaf.html> (June 8, 2006).

16. International Food Policy Research Institute, "New Study Debunks Misconceptions about Biotech Crop Research in Africa," press release, July 13, 2005, <http://www.ifpri.org/PRESSREL/2005/20050713.htm> (May 25, 2006).

17. Ibid.; see also Idah Sithole-Niang1, Joel Cohen, and Patricia Zambrano, "Putting GM Technologies to Work: Public Research Pipelines in Selected African Countries," *African Journal of Biotechnology,* November 2004, pp. 564–571, <http://www.ifpri.org/pubs/articles/2004/africajbiotech.pdf> (June 8, 2006).

18. Jikun Huang, Ruifa Hu, Scott Rozelle, and Carl Pray, "Insect-Resistant GM Rice in Farmers' Fields: Assessing Productivity and Health Effects in China," *Science,* April 29, 2005, pp. 688–690.

19. "Genetically Modified Rice In China Benefits Farmers' Health, Study Finds," *ScienceDaily,* news release, April 28, 2005, <http://www.sciencedaily.com/releases/2005/04/050428181133.htm> (May 25, 2006).

20. Arlene Weintraub, "What's So Scary About Rice?" *Business Week,* August 1, 2005, p. 58.

Chapter 6   Regulating GE Crops

1. Friends of the Earth, "GM Crop Safety Tests 'Flawed,' New Scientific Paper Shows," news release, November 16, 2004, <http://www.foe.org/new/releases/1104gmcrops.html> (May 25, 2006).

2. Alan McHughen, "Plant Genetic Engineering and Regulation in the United States," Agricultural Biotechnology In California Series Publication 8179, n.d., <http://anrcatalog.ucdavis.edu/pdf/8179.pdf> (May 24, 2006).

3. The United States Mission to the European Union, "Fact Sheets: U.S. Request for WTO Consultations on EU Biotech Moratorium," May 13, 2003, <http://www.useu.be/Categories/Biotech/May1303BiotechFactSheets.html> (May 25, 2006).

4. Michael R. Taylor, Jody S. Tick, Diane M. Sherman, "Tending the Fields: State & Federal Roles in the Oversight of Genetically Modified Crops," A report commissioned by the Pew Initiative on Food and Biotechnology and prepared by Resources for the Future, December 2004, p. 27.

5. Ibid., p. 29.

6. World Public Opinion.org, "Biotechnology—Labeling GM Foods," 2003, <http://www.americans-world.org/digest/global_issues/biotechnology/biotech3.cfm (May 24, 2006).

7. Eric Kelderman, "Alaska to Label Biotech Fish," *Stateline.org,* June 15, 2005, <http://www.stateline.org/live/ViewPage.action?site NodeId=136&languageId=1&contentId=37510> (June 8, 2006).

8. Hal Spence, "Bill Requires Labeling Genetically Altered Fish," *Peninsula Clarion,* May 8, 2005, <http://www.peninsulaclarion.com/stories/050805/news_0508new004001.shtml> (June 8, 2006).

9. Union of Concerned Scientists, "Genetically Engineered Salmon," February 1, 2001, <http://www.ucsusa.org/food_and_environment/genetic_engineering/genetically-engineered-salmon.html> (May 25, 2006).

10. "Background: Industry Aims to Strip Local Control of Food Supply," *environmentalcommons.org,* n.d., <http://environmental commons.org/seedlawbackgrounder.html> (May 25, 2006).

11. "Europeans, Science and Technology," *Eurobarometer 55.2,* December 2001, <http://ec.europa.eu/research/press/2001/pr0612 en-report.pdf> (May 24, 2006).

12. Pew Initiative on Food and Biotechnology, "U.S. vs. EU: An Examination of the Trade Issues Surrounding Genetically Modified Food," August 2003, <http://pewagbiotech.org/resources/issue briefs/europe.pdf> (May 24, 2006).

13. Elisabeth Rosenthal, "Biotech Food Tears Rift in Europe," *New York Times,* June 6, 2006, <http://www.nytimes.com/2006/06/06/business/worldbusiness/06gene.html?ex=1162180800&en=3b8abc 953690906d&ei=5070> (October 28, 2006).

14. Center for Food Safety, "Genetically Engineered Crops and Foods: Regional Regulation and Prohibition," July 2005, <http://www.

centerforfoodsafety.org/pubs/Regional%20Chart.pdf> (June 8, 2006).

Chapter 7   The Politics of GMOs

1. Guy Cook, *Genetically Modified Language* (London and New York: Routledge, 20045), p. 112.
2. Ibid., frontispiece.
3. Bill Lambrecht, *Dinner at the New Gene Café* (New York: St. Martin's Griffin, 2001), p. 234.
4. Peter Pringle, *Food, Inc.: Mendel to Monsanto—The Promises and Perils of the Biotech Harvest* (New York: Simon & Schuster, 2003), p. 21.
5. Jim Greenwood, "Testimony Regarding Benefits and Future Developments in Agriculture and Food Biotechnology," June 14, 2005, <http://www.bio.org/foodag/action/20050614.asp> (June 8, 2006).
6. "About Agbioworld," n.d., <http://www.agbioworld.org/about/index.html> (June 8, 2006).
7. Lambrecht, p. 269.
8. Christian Aid, "Selling Suicide—Farming, False Promises and Genetic Engineering In Developing Countries," May 1999, <http://www.christian-aid.org.uk/indepth/9905suic/suicide2.htm#biotechnology> (May 25, 2006).
9. "Grocery Store Wars," Organic Trade Association, n.d., <http://www.storewars.org> (June 16, 2006).
10. Ronnie Cummins, "Food's High Prices Proven Healthy," Knight Ridder, August 14, 2005, <http://www.etaiwannews.com/Opinion/2005/08/14/112398> (August 15, 2005).
11. "Current Organic Agricultural Market Worldwide: A Year in View (2005)," <http://www.researchandmarkets.com/feats/download_pdf.asp?report_id> (June 8, 2006).

Chapter 8   Consumer Views and Choices

1. National Consumer Council, "GM Food The Consumer Interest,"

n.d., <http://www.ncc.org.uk/policy/gm_at_glance.pdf> (June 8, 2006).

2. Edie Lau, "Grocery Quandary," Part 5 of "Seeds of Doubt," *Sacramento Bee*, June 10, 2004, <http://www.sacbee.com/static/live/news/projects/biotech/c5_1.html> (June 8, 2006).

3. "Talks on GM Labels Stalled at Codex Meeting," *Food Production Daily*, May 18, 2005, Checkbiotech.org, <http://www.checkbiotech.org/root/index.cfm?fuseaction=search&search=Codex%20meeting&doc_id=10349&start=1&fullsearch=0> (June 8, 2006).

4. "What's in it for you? Genetically Modified Food: The New European GM Labelling And Traceability Regulations," *Agricultural Biotechnology Europe*, Spring 2004, <http://www.eubusiness.com/guides/GM_Labelling_Guide_Eng.pdf> (May 24, 2006).

5. Pew Initiative on Food and Biotechnology, "Overview of Findings 2004 Focus Groups & Poll," n.d., <http://pewagbiotech.org/research/2004update/overview.pdf> (May 24, 2006).

6. Pew Initiative on Food and Biotechnology, "Is Labeling GM Foods an Effective Means of Facilitating Choices for Consumers?" August 28, 2002, <http://pewagbiotech.org/buzz/display.php3?StoryID=73> (May 25, 2006).

7. Karma Metzgar, "Why the Little Sticky Label on Fruit?" University of Missouri Extension, n.d., <http://missourifamilies.org/features/nutritionarticles/nut76.htm>; Marion Owen, "Talking Fruit: How to De-code the Information On Those Little Stickers," n.d., <http://www.plantea.com/genetically-modified-foods.htm>; and "Organic Foods and GE," n.d., <http://www.innvista.com/HEALTH/foods/geneteng/organic.htm> (May 24, 2006).

8. "Trader Joe's Stance on Genetically Modified Foods," March 31, 2003, <http://www.traderjoes.com/new/gmf.asp> (June 8, 2006).

9. The True Food Network, "The True Food Shopping Guide," n.d., <http://www.truefoodnow.org/shoppersguide/index.html> (June 8, 2006).

Glossary

agbiotech—A term for agricultural biotechnology.

agribusiness—A large multinational corporation that manufactures a variety of agricultural products.

Bacillus thuringiensis (**Bt**)—An insecticidal toxin.

biotechnology—The manipulation of organisms for a human purpose.

chromosome—A sequence of DNA that carries genetic information.

DNA (deoxyribonucleic acid)—Four small chemical bases linked together in long chains; a specific set of base pairs on a DNA strand makes up a gene.

Environmental Protection Agency (EPA)—A federal agency that is responsible for protecting the environment by controlling air and water pollution, radiation, pesticide hazards, and solid waste disposal and for conducting ecological research.

enzymes—Proteins that regulate a chemical reaction.

European Union (EU)—A coalition of twenty-five independent European countries established to unite European nations economically and politically and to reduce trade barriers.

Food and Drug Administration (FDA)—A division of the U.S. Department of Health and Human Services that regulates human and animal food, drugs, and medical devices; dietary supplements; cosmetics; and blood products.

gene—A unit of heredity.

"gene gun"—A device scientists use to transfer genes to an organism's cells.

genetic engineering—Inserting a gene or genes from one organism into another.

genetic modification—A term used to indicate the insertion of DNA from one organism to another.

genetically modified organism (GMO)—An organism that is the result of genetic modification.

glyphosphate—A herbicide, or weed killer.

hybrid—An organism created from crossbreeding.

living modified organism—Another term for a GMO.

marker gene—A gene that allows genetically modified cells to be readily selected.

pharma crops—Crops genetically modified to contain medicinals or industrial chemicals.

proteins—Chemicals that provide structure and physical characteristics, or regulate chemical reactions in an organism.

recombinant DNA (rDNA)—Pieces of DNA that have been spliced together, usually using specialized enzymes.

toxin—A poison.

transgenic—Adjective for an organism carrying artificially inserted genetic material.

U.S. Department of Agriculture (USDA)—An agency that develops agricultural and food policies, promotes agricultural trade, and protects food safety and natural resources.

World Trade Organization (WTO)—An international agency that governs trade between member nations and resolves trade disputes when they arise.

For More Information

Council for Biotechnology Information
1225 Eye Street, NW
Suite 400
Washington, D.C. 20005
Phone: 202-962-9200

The Pew Initiative on Food and Biotechnology
1331 H Street
Suite 900
Washington, D.C. 20005
Phone: 202-347-9044

Rutgers University Food Policy Institute
3 Rutgers Plaza
New Brunswick, N.J. 08901
Phone: 732-932-1966

Union of Concerned Scientists
2 Brattle Square
Cambridge, Mass. 02238-9105
Phone: 617-547-5552

United States Department of Agriculture
1400 Independence Ave., SW
Washington, D.C. 20250
Phone: 202-720-2791

Further Reading

Books

Cothran, Helen, editor. *Global Resources: Opposing Viewpoints.* San Diego, Calif.: Greenhaven Press, 2003.

Harris, Nancy, editor. *Genetically Engineered Food.* San Diego, Calif.: Greenhaven Press, 2004.

Hart, Kathleen. *Eating in the Dark: America's Experiment With Genetically Engineered Food.* New York: Random House/ Vintage, 2002.

Kowalski, Kathiann M. *The Debate Over Genetically Engineered Food: Healthy or Harmful?* Berkeley Heights, N.J.: Enslow Publishers, Inc., 2002.

Morris, Jonathan. *The Ethics of Biotechnology.* Philadelphia: Chelsea House, 2005.

Schmaefsky, Brian. *Biotechnology on the Farm and in the Factory: Agricultural and Industrial Applications.* Philadelphia: Chelsea House, 2006.

Internet Addresses

AgBioWorld
   <http://www.agbioworld.org>

Center for Food Safety
   <http://www.centerforfoodsafety.org>

Friends of the Earth
   <http://www.foe.org>

Monsanto Company
   <http://www.monsanto.com/monsanto/layout/ default.asp>

Index

A

agbiotech companies, 29, 32, 40, 47, 54, 67, 77–79, 81
AgBioWorld, 80
American Farm Bureau, 55
American Medical Association, 13, 55
American Soybean Association (ASA), 55, 79
antibiotics, 25, 39, 44, 83
antioxidants, 26
Aqua Bounty Technologies, 71
artificial insemination, 25
Aventis CropScience, 50

B

bacteria, 12, 14, 18, 25, 32
BASF, 29
Bayer, 29
beta-carotene, 26, 77–79
Biodemocracy, 39
biodiversity, 75
Bioengineering Action Network, 39
biotech, 8–9, 28, 30, 40, 42, 55–56, 59–60, 62, 69, 76, 78–80
biotechnology, 9, 11, 17, 25, 28–29, 40, 56, 80
    companies, 79
    conference, 60
    developments, 79
    revolution, 60
Biotechnology Industry Organization (BIO), 40, 55, 79–80
bollworm, 58
bovine growth hormone (bgh), 13
bovine somatotropin (bST), 13
Bt crops, 14–15, 28, 42, 45, 47–49, 56, 58, 60, 67

C

Calgene, 16

canola, 16, 27–28, 30, 34–35, 55, 75, 88, 93
Cartagena Protocol, 67, 75
Center for Food Safety (CFS), 33
Centers for Disease Control and Protection (CDC), 50
Christian Aid, 40–41, 81
Christian Science Monitor, 61
Congress of Racial Equality (CORE), 59–60
Conservation Technology Information Center, 58
conservation tillage, 58–59
Council for Agricultural Science and Technology, 58
Council for Biotechnology Information (CBI), 54–56
CropLife America, 55

D

Declaration of Scientists in Support of Biotechnology, 80
deoxyribonucleic acid (DNA), 9, 11–13, 16, 32, 54, 83
Dow, 29, 32, 36
DuPont, 23, 29, 32, 36

E

EarthSave, 39
ecologists, 71
edible vaccines, 63
embryos, 12–13
Enviropig, 7–8, 12, 13
enzyme, 12–13
Escherichia coli (E. coli), 12
Eurobarometer, 72
European Union (EU), 39, 40, 67, 73, 85

F

Federal Food, Drug, and Cosmetic Act, 67

Federal Insecticide, Fungicide, and
    Rodenticide Act, 67
fermentation, 9, 17–18
Flavr Savr tomato, 15
Food and Agricultural Organization of
    the United Nations, 55
Food, Inc., 78
Food Policy Institute (FPI), 9, 12
foot-and-mouth disease, 73
Frankenfoods, 38
Friends of the Earth, 39, 68, 82

G

General Agreement on Tariffs and
    Trade (GATT), 73
Genetically Modified Language, 76
genetically modified organisms
    (GMOs), 9, 36–37, 39–40, 42,
    53–55, 66, 68, 72–75, 76, 77, 79,
    81–82, 86–87, 90, 93
genetic use restriction technologies
    (GURT), 41, 42
gene transfer, 11–13
GeneWatch UK, 45
golden rice, 78
greenhouse gases, 59
Greenpeace International, 45
Grocery Manufacturers of America,
    55, 90

H

herbicide tolerant, 28, 42, 58–59
hog farms, 7–8
hybrid(s), 22–23, 48

I

Incas, 19
indigenous people, 18
insecticides, 14, 25, 29, 56
insect resistant, 28, 63
International Food Policy Research
    Institute (IFPRI), 62
International Society of African
    Scientists, 55

M

mad cow disease, 72
maize, 18, 39, 45–46, 47, 48, 60, 61,
    62
marker genes, 39
Mendel, Gregor, 20–22
molds, 18
monarch butterfly, 47–48
Monsanto, 29, 30, 32–36, 41, 55

N

National Academy of Sciences, 44, 48
National Center for Food and
    Agricultural Policy (NCFAP), 55,
    58
National Consumer Council (NCC),
    86
National Corn Growers Association
    (NCGA), 55, 56
National Cotton Council (NCC), 55
Nature, 45–48
New York Times, 73

O

Online NewsHour, 8
organic, 26, 42, 44, 69, 82–83, 85, 91,
    93
Organic Consumers Association
    (OCA), 83
Organization for Economic
    Cooperation and Development, 55

P

patent, 32, 33–36, 41, 42
pesticides, 14, 23, 26, 29, 44, 53, 58,
    62–63, 83
Pew Initiative on Food and
    Biotechnology, 28, 69, 88
pharma crops, 50–52, 63–65, 67
phosphorous, 8, 13
phytase, 13
plant breeder(s), 20, 23
Plant Variety Patent (PVP), 32
pollen, 18, 21, 44, 47–48, 85

Price, Carlyle, 33–34
Proceedings of the Royal Society of London, 48
processed food(s), 16, 26, 37, 39, 46, 51, 85, 90, 93
ProdiGene, 51–52
proteins, 11, 63, 65

R

rapeseed, 16, 27, 34, 39, 48–49, 75, 93
recombinant bovine somatotropin (rbst), 13
Riceland Foods, 52
Roundup Ready (RR), 30, 32–35

S

Say No to GMOs, 39
Schmeiser, Percy, 34–35
Selling Suicide, 41, 81
Sierra Club, 39, 82
StarLink, 49–50
Store Wars: the Organic Rebellion, 82, 83
streptomycin, 25
suicide seeds, 38, 41–42
Syngenta, 29, 32, 36, 39, 78

T

terminator technology, 41–42
Toxic Substances Control Act, 67
Trader Joe's, 93
transgenic technology, 9
True Foods Campaign, 39–40
Truth about Trade and Technology, 55

U

Union of Concerned Scientists (UCS), 42, 48, 71
U.S. Department of Agriculture (USDA), 41–42, 51, 67, 79, 83
U.S. Environmental Protection Agency (EPA), 14, 49, 67, 79

V

Ventria Biosciences, 52, 63
Voices from Africa: Biotechnology and the Subsistence Farmer, 60

W

Wallace, Henry, 23
Whole Foods, 93
World Health Organization, 54–55, 87, 90
World Trade Organization (WTO), 40, 67, 73